Adult Coloring Book

ANIMAL KINGDOM

Book 1: Mi

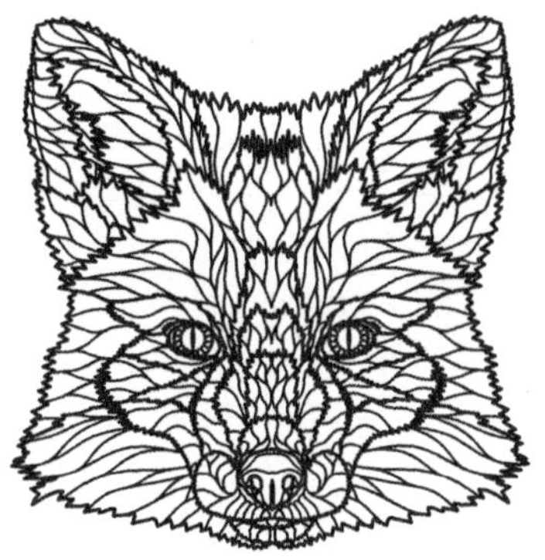

Illustrations

Tomasz Kuberski

Publishing

Fine Lines Books

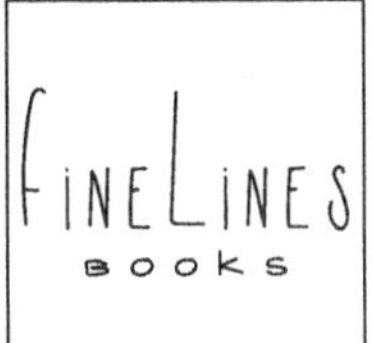

www.finelinesbooks.com

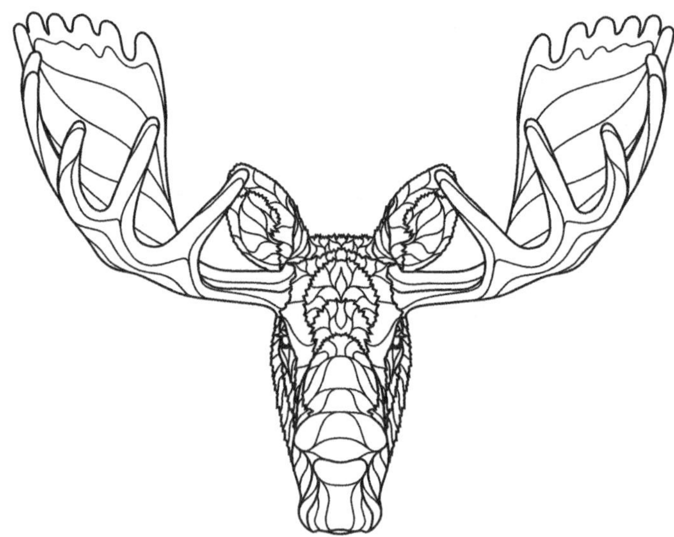

Dear Colorist,

Thank you for choosing our coloring book "Mind", the first in our Animal Kingdom series.

Within this book you will find:

- Original illustrations created specifically for this book.
- Two styles for each image. The first image in each section is not restricted by interior markings, allowing you the freedom of expression within your coloring whilst the second image uses thin interior lines that are designed in such a way that you can either do individual block/cell coloring or use them as a guide to simulate fur or skin texture on your chosen animal.
- Specially considered illustration placement to allow for a double blank page between images and also to assist with guidance when coloring the less defined picture.

⚠ To avoid bleeding through the pages, especially when use felt or paint pens, we strongly recommend using card or a plastic sheet underneath the page.

If you like our book, please leave a review on Amazon.

To receive news, ideas and other coloring related tips and tricks please sign up to our email list at www.finelinesbooks.com.

We hope you enjoy coloring each illustration and the animal head designs inspire your artistic flair. We encourage you to display your creations and we would love to see your interpretations on our Facebook page. To find us, please scan the QR code on the back cover or visit our website.

Yours truly
The Fine Lines Team

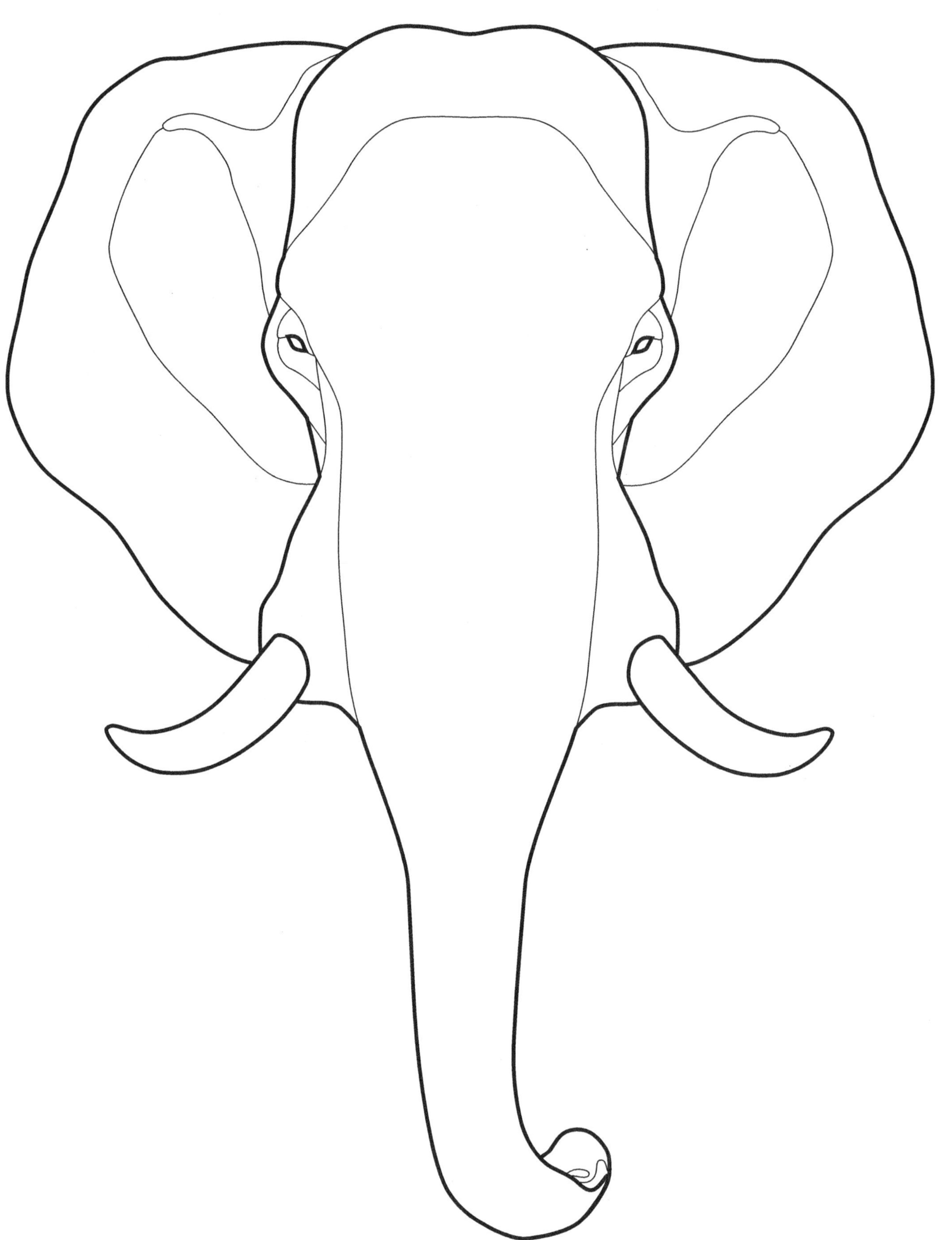

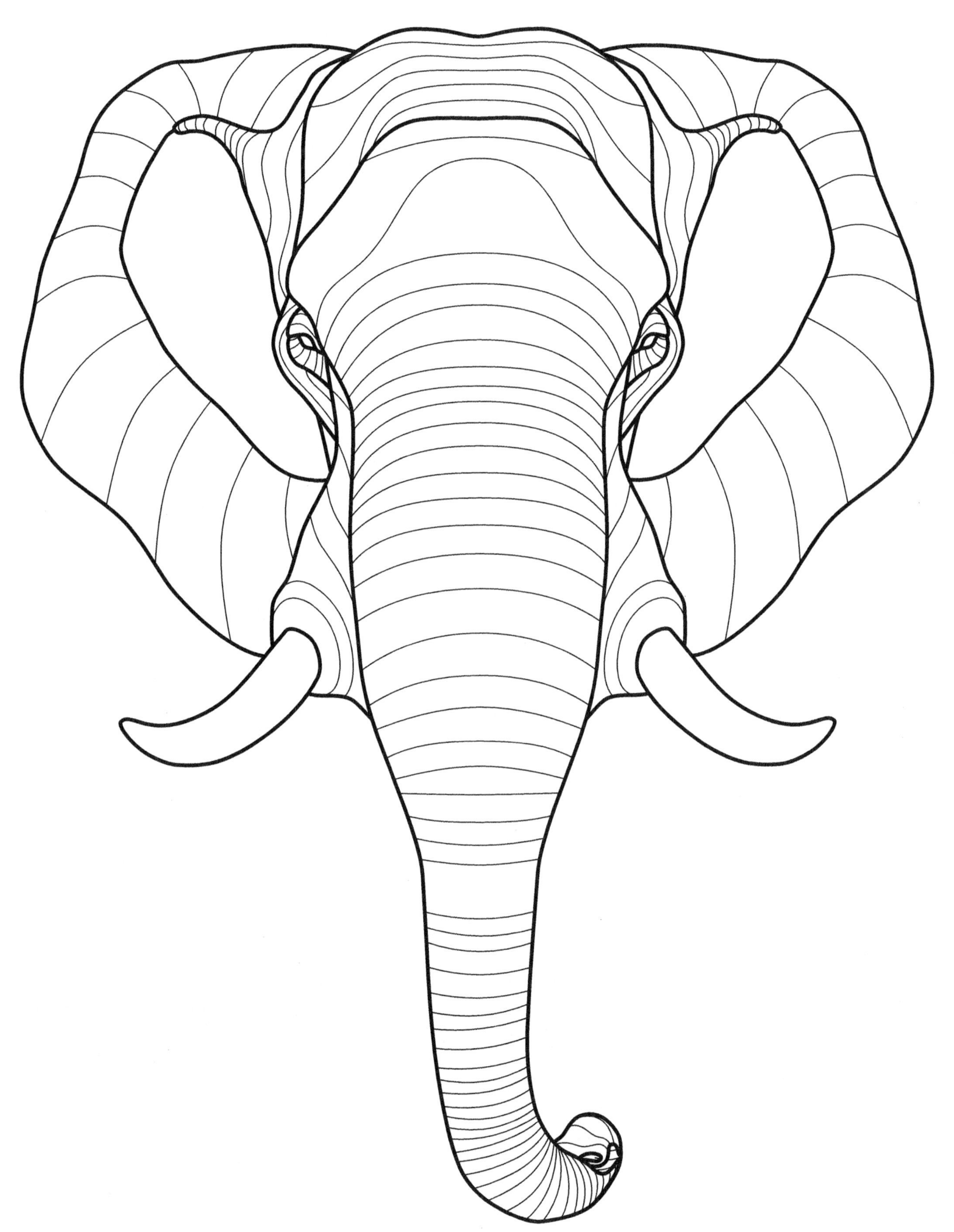

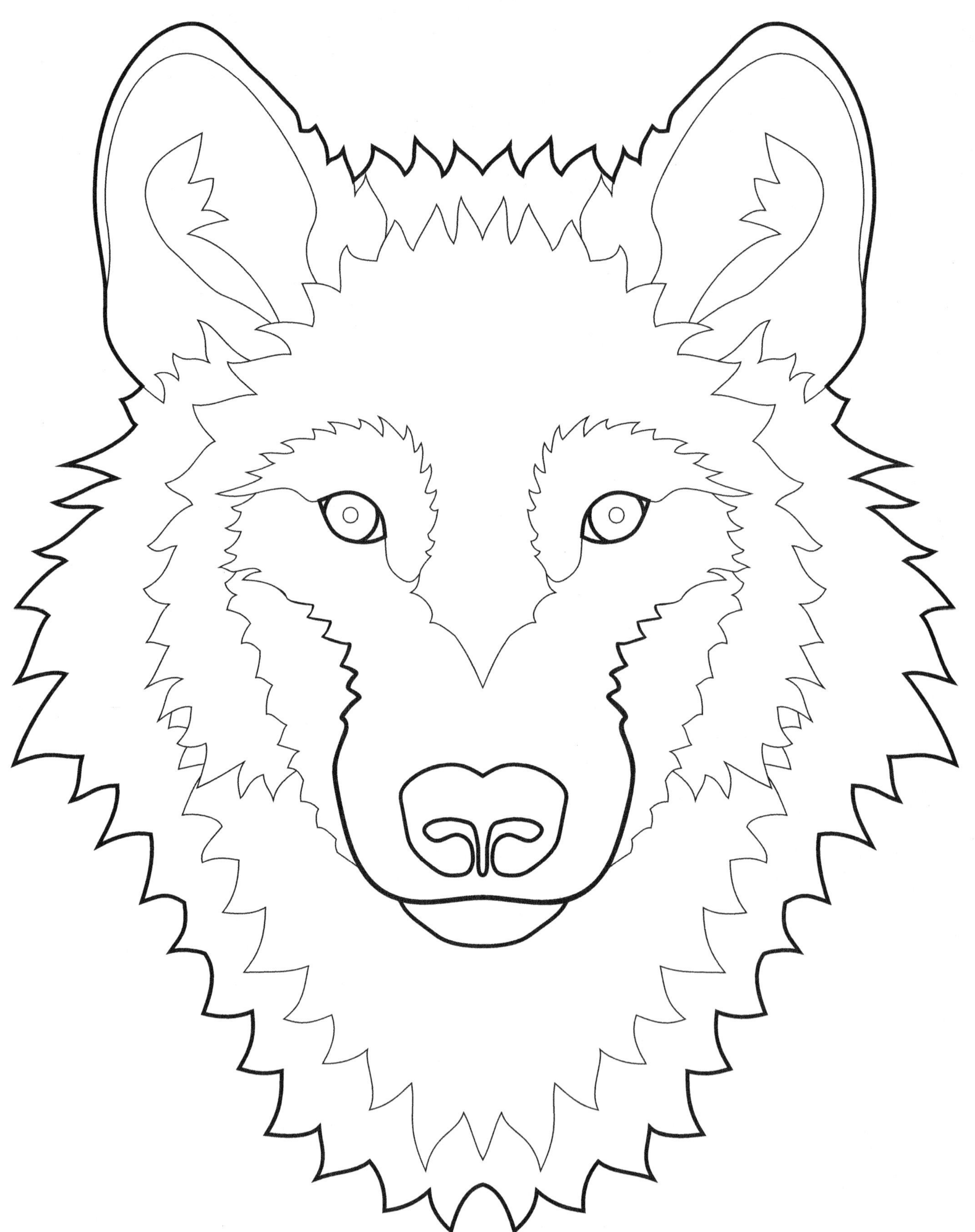

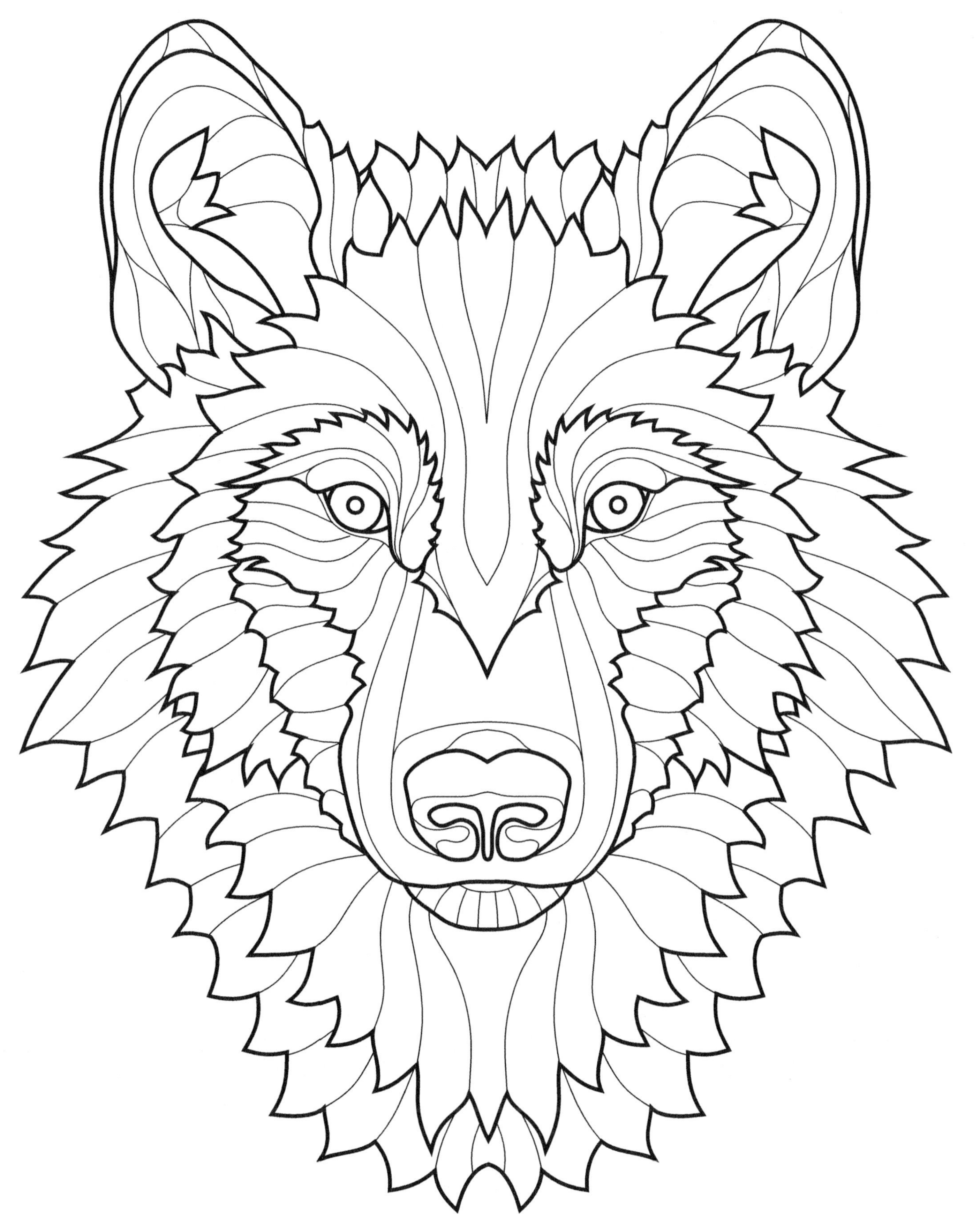

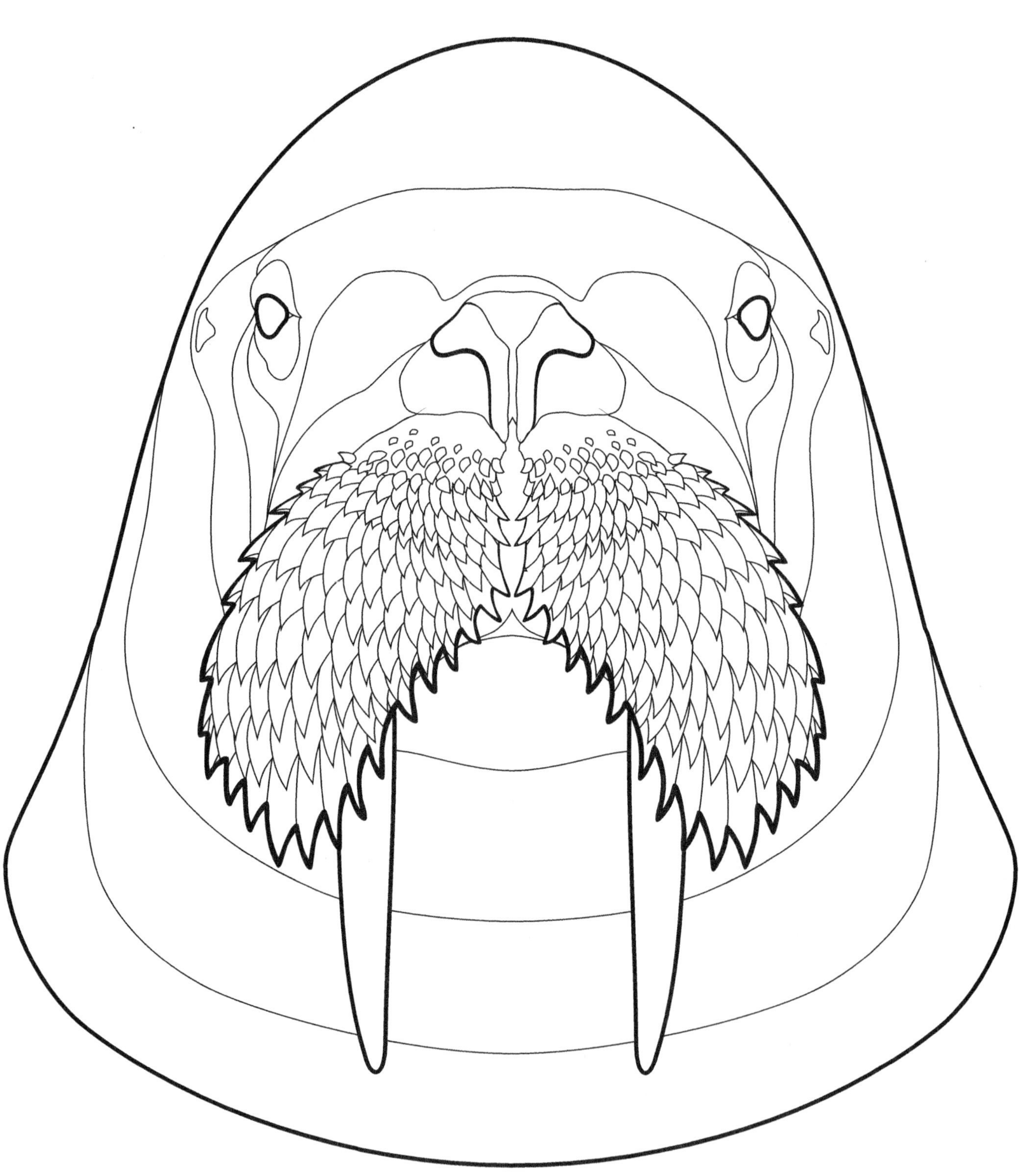

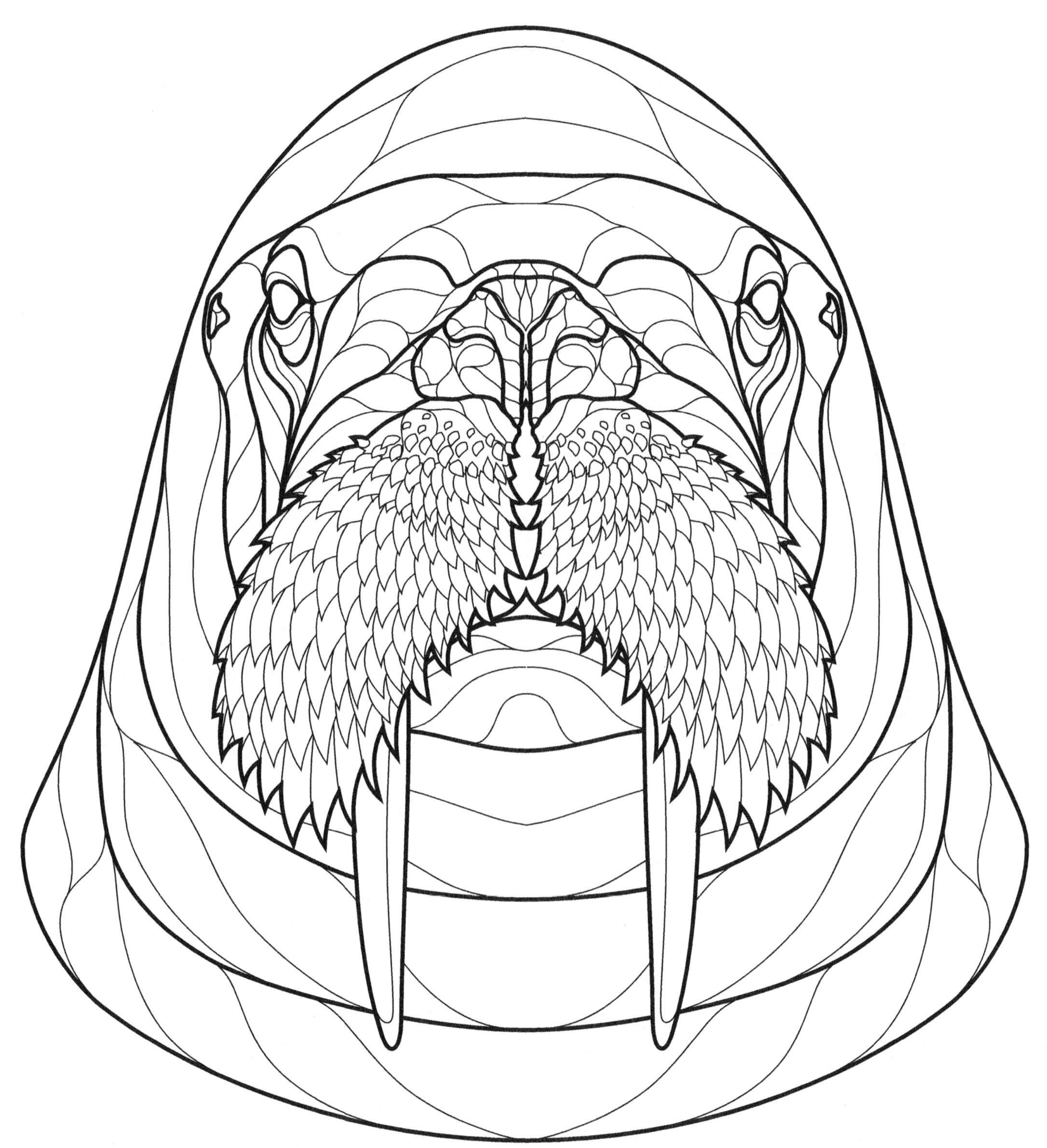

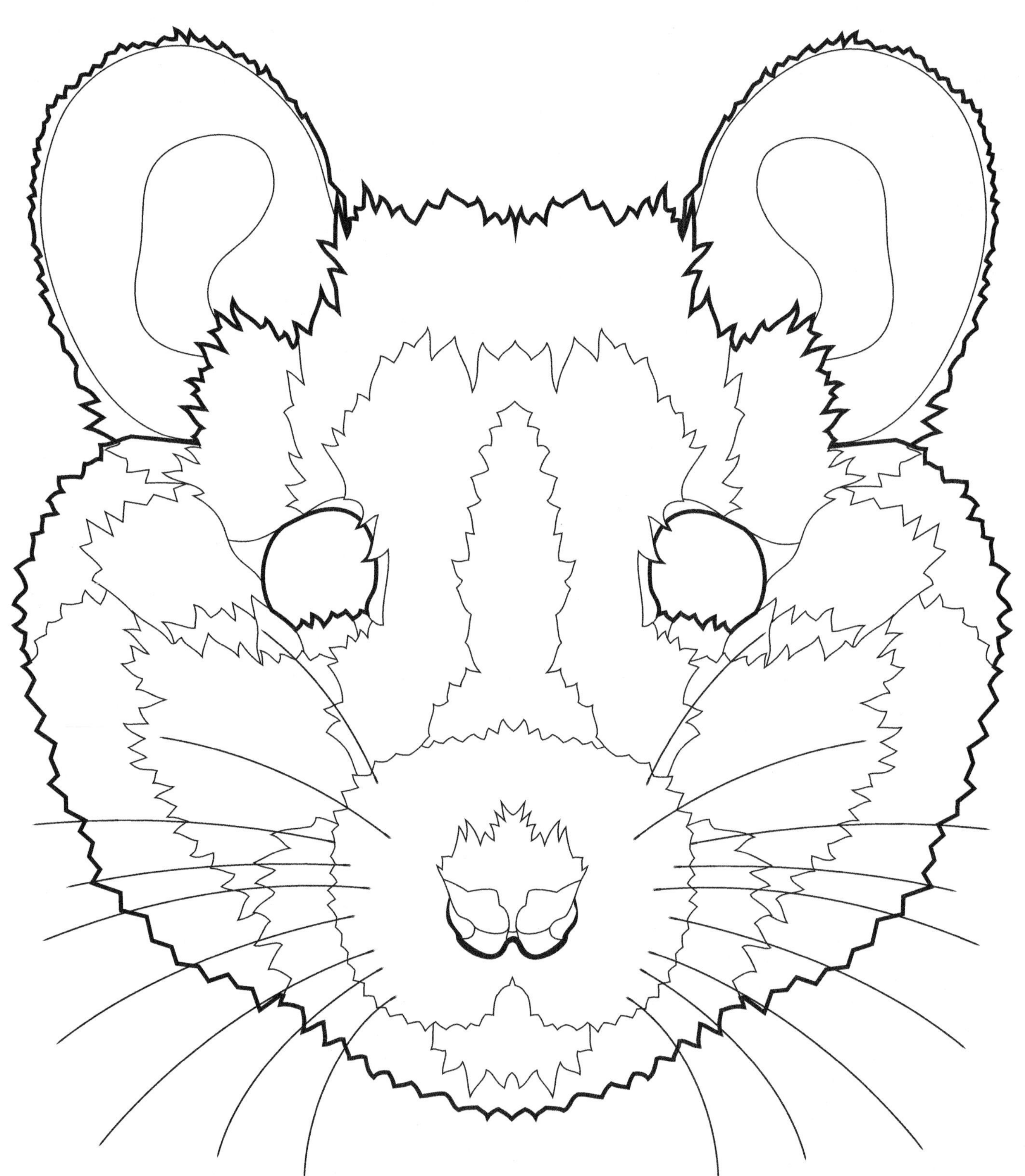

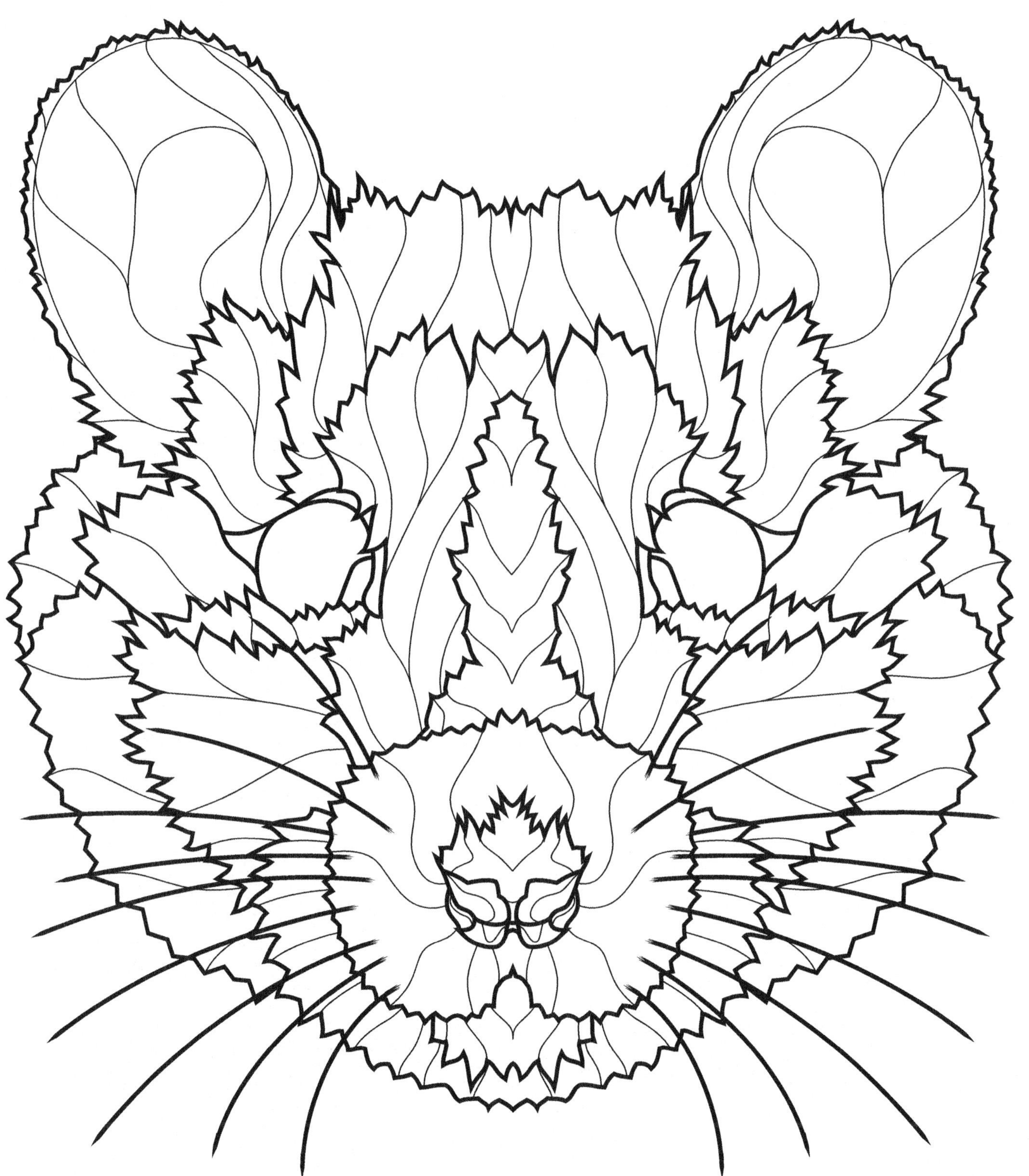

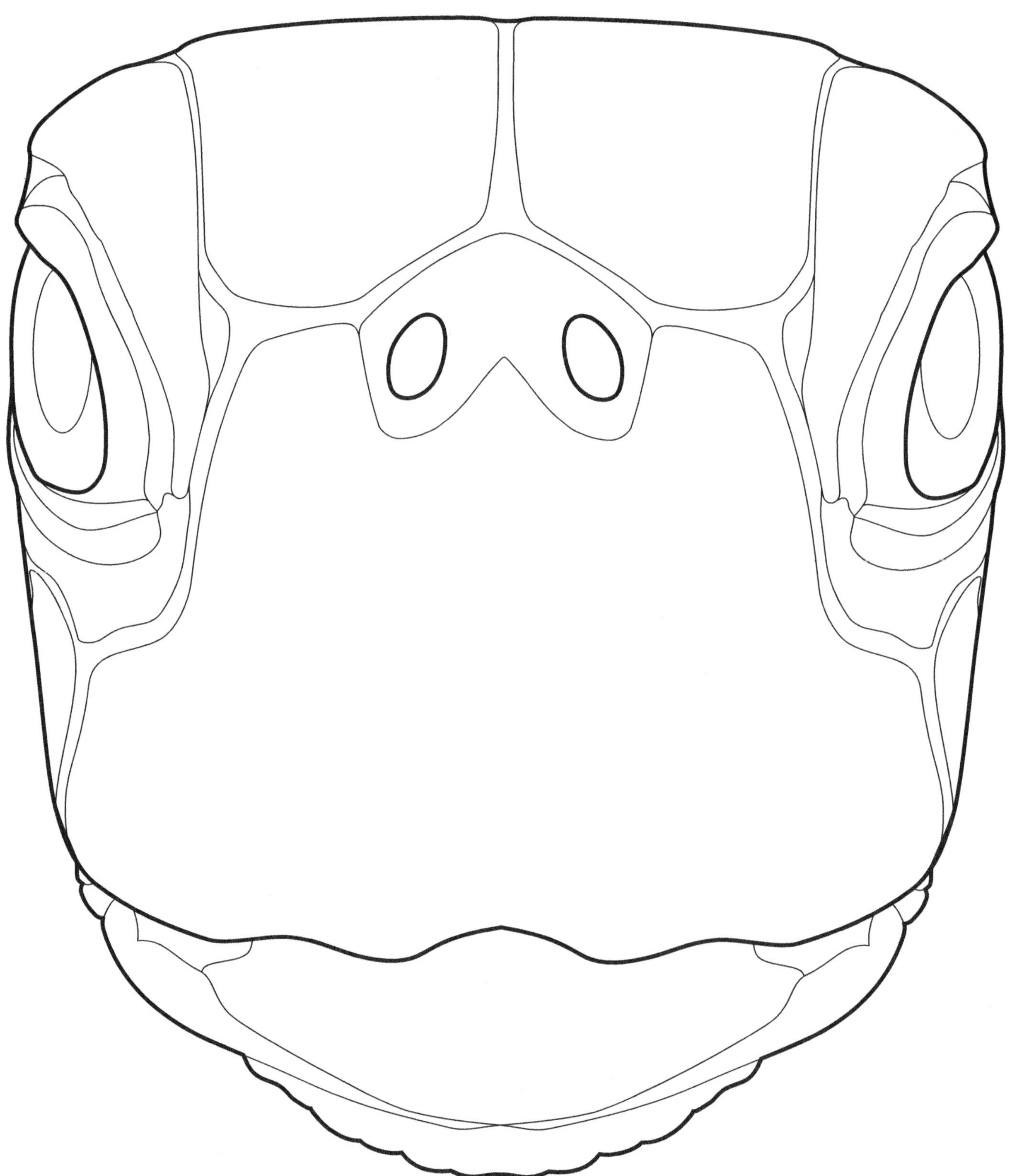

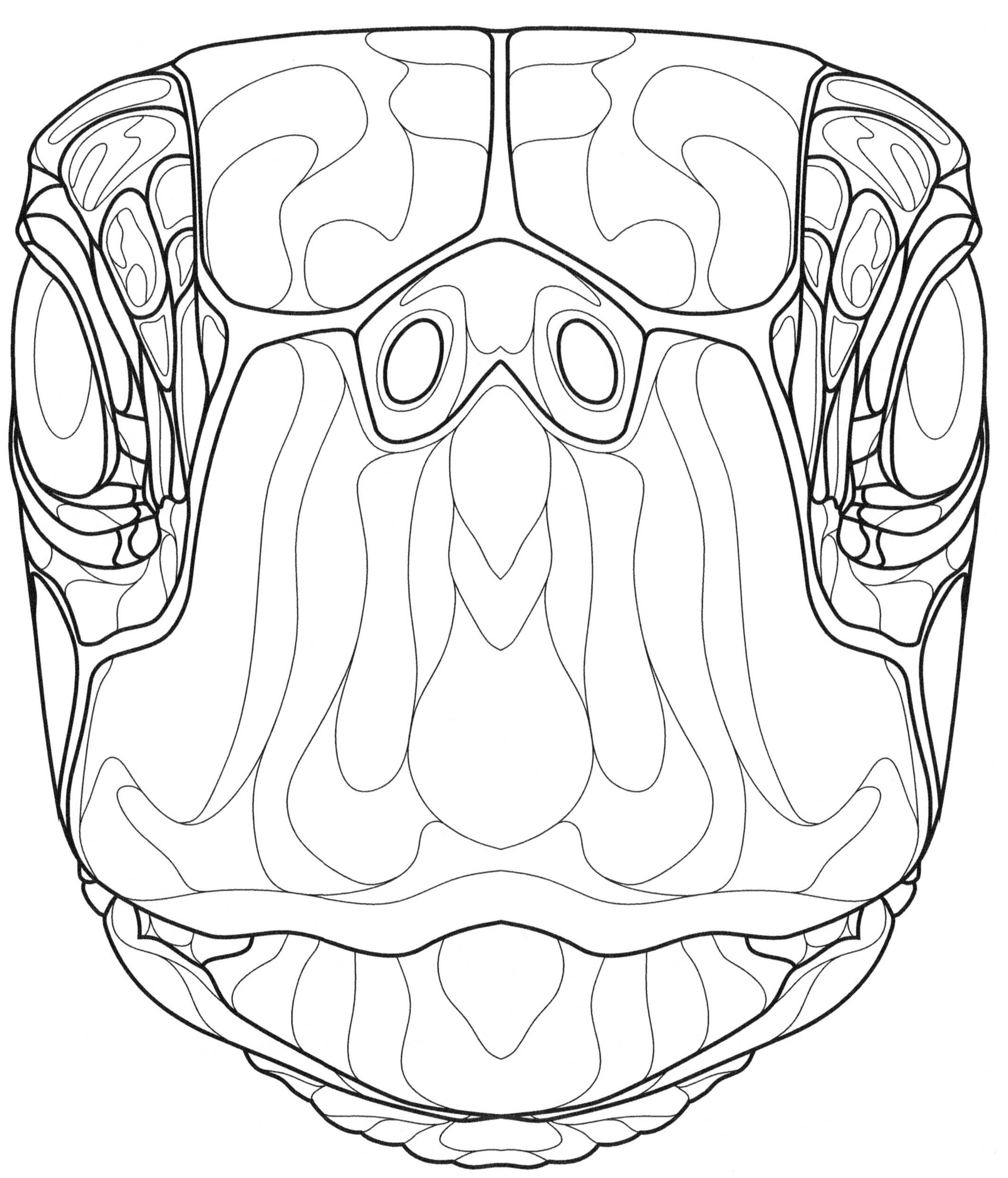

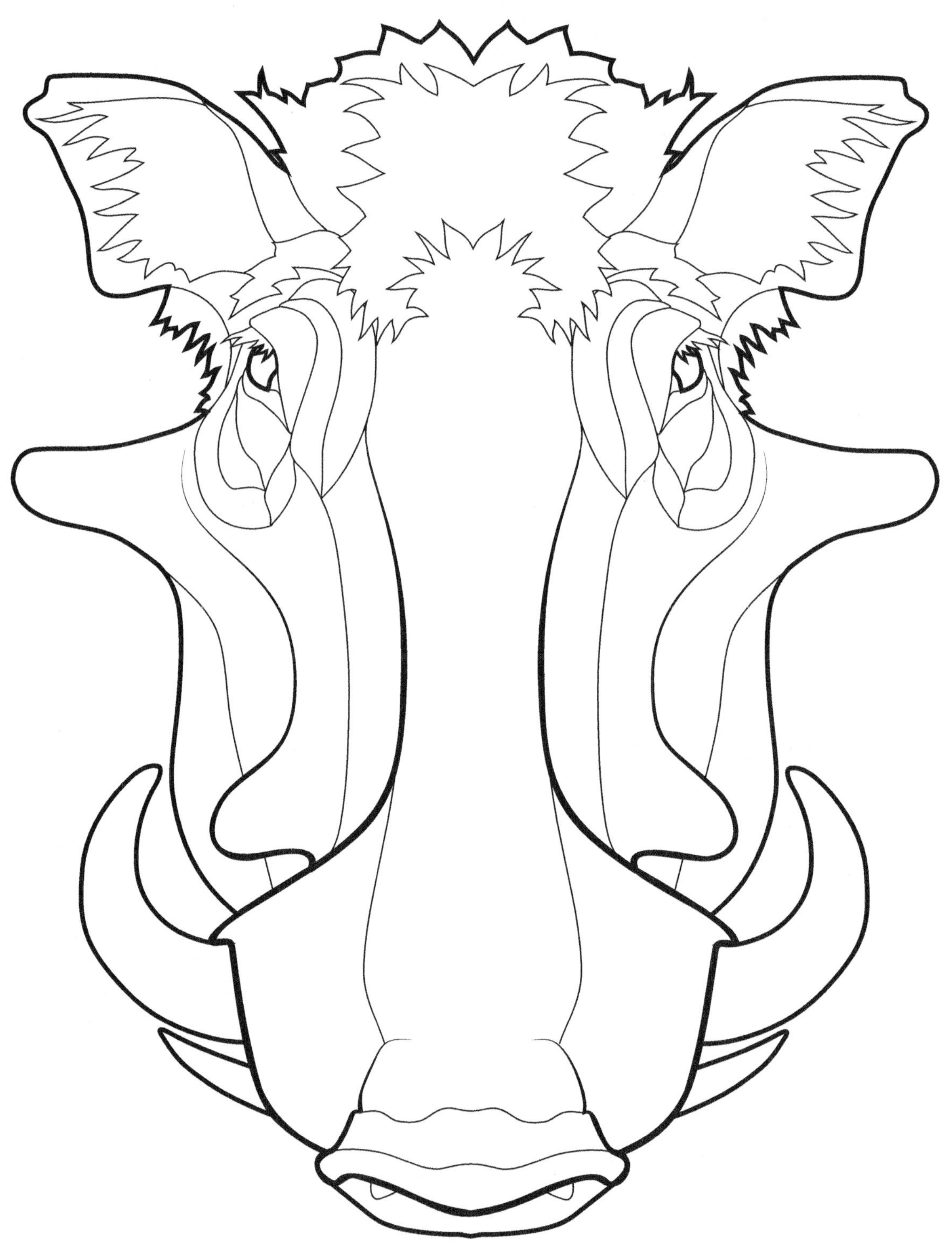

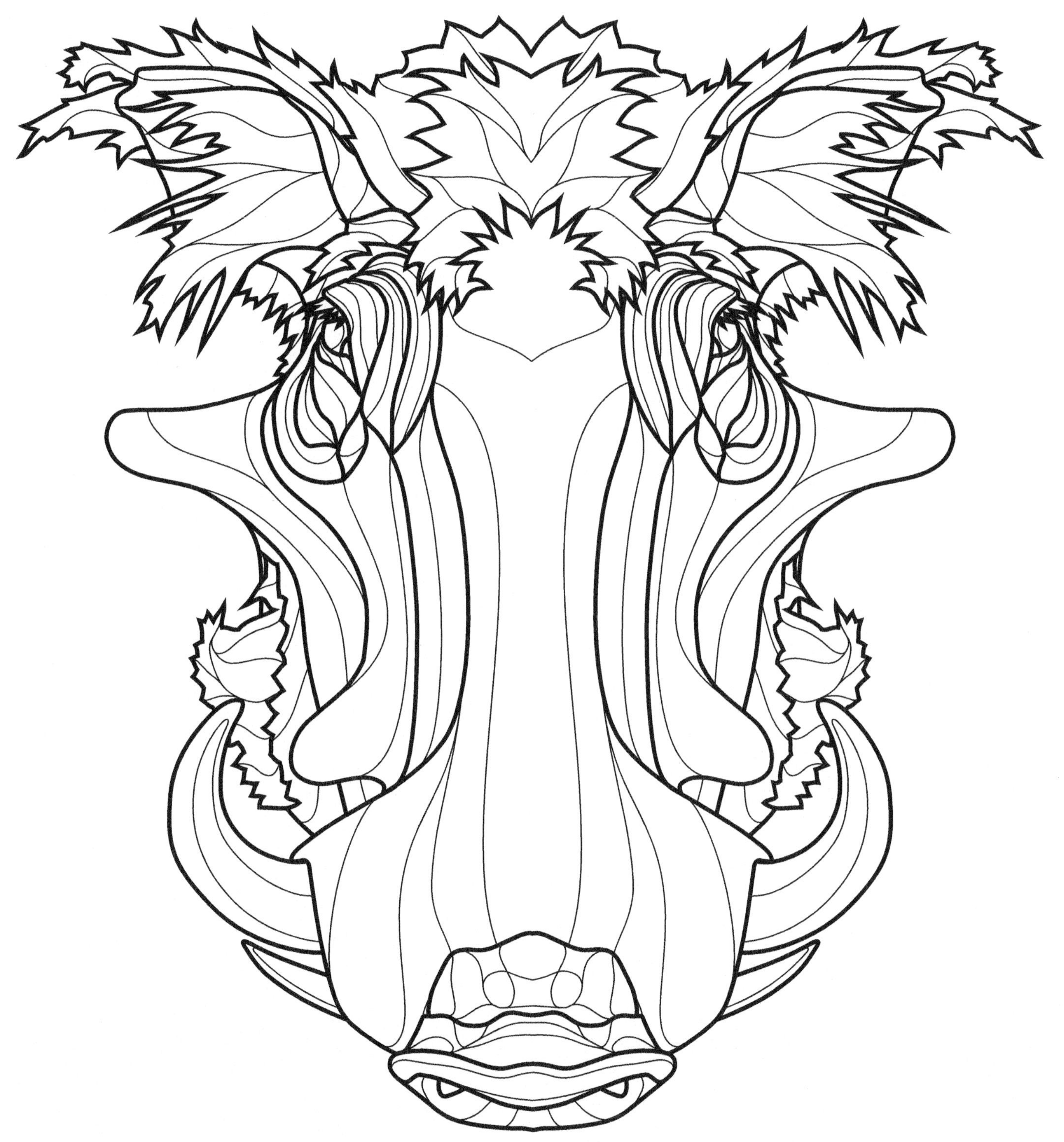

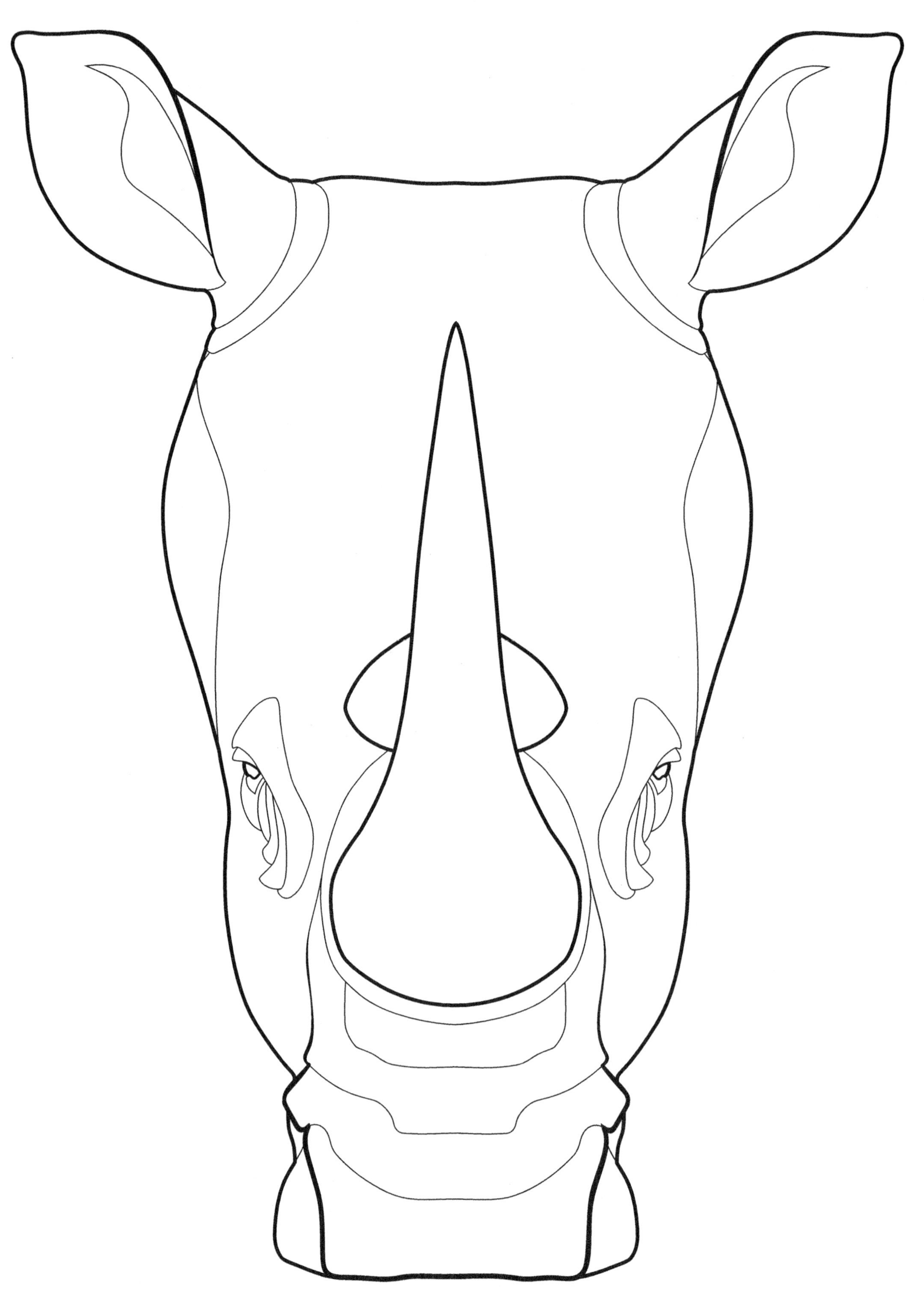

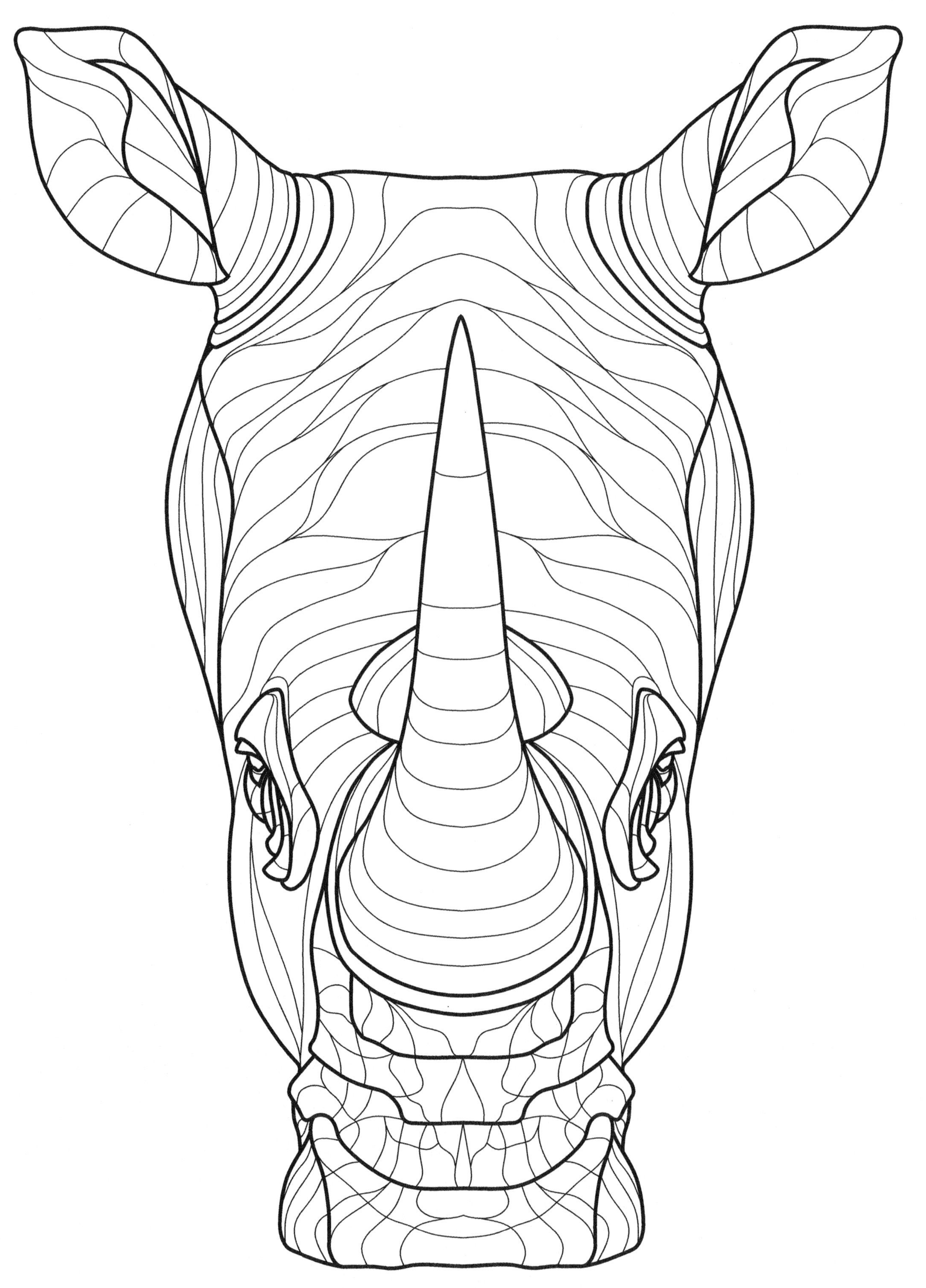

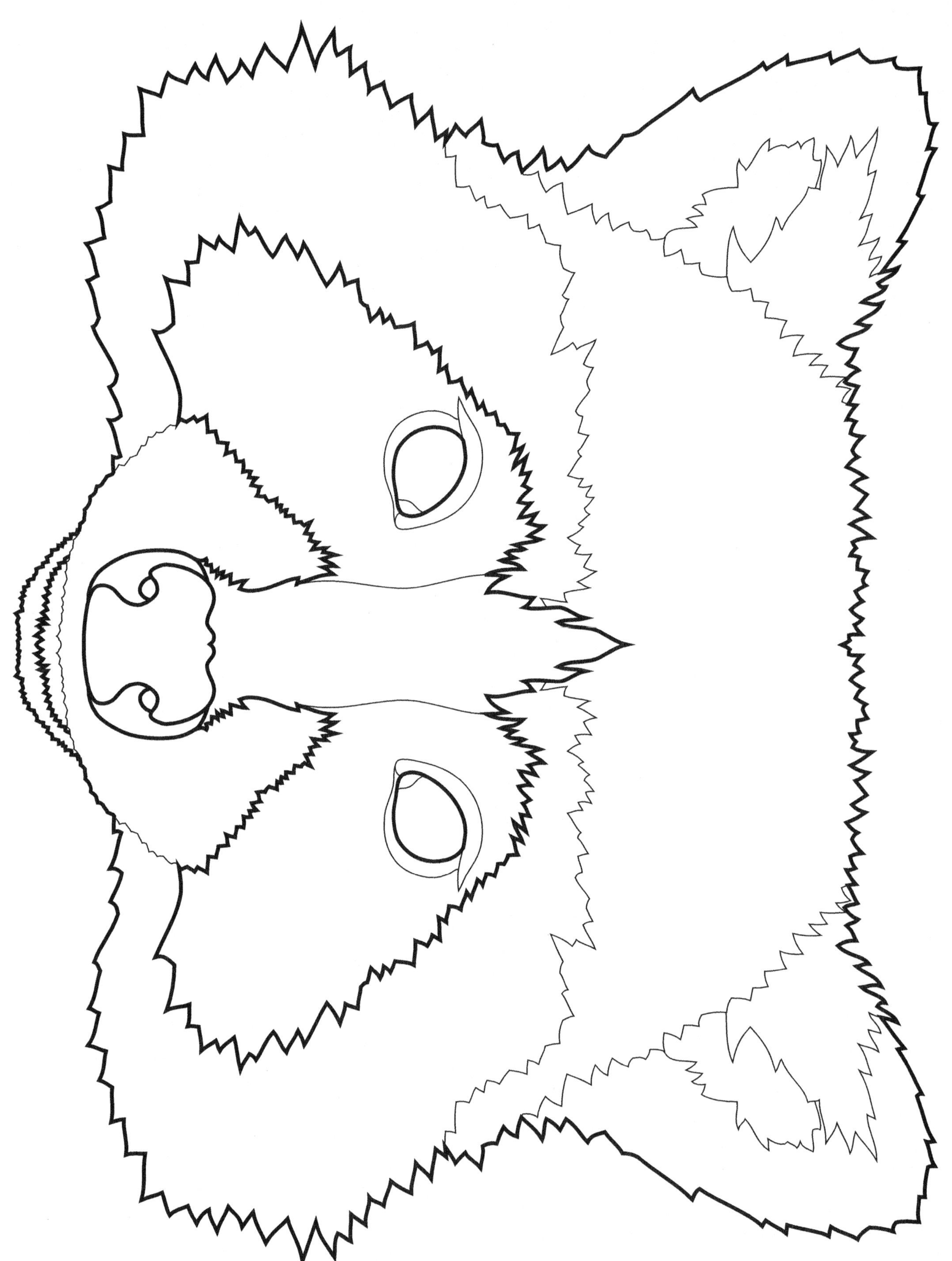

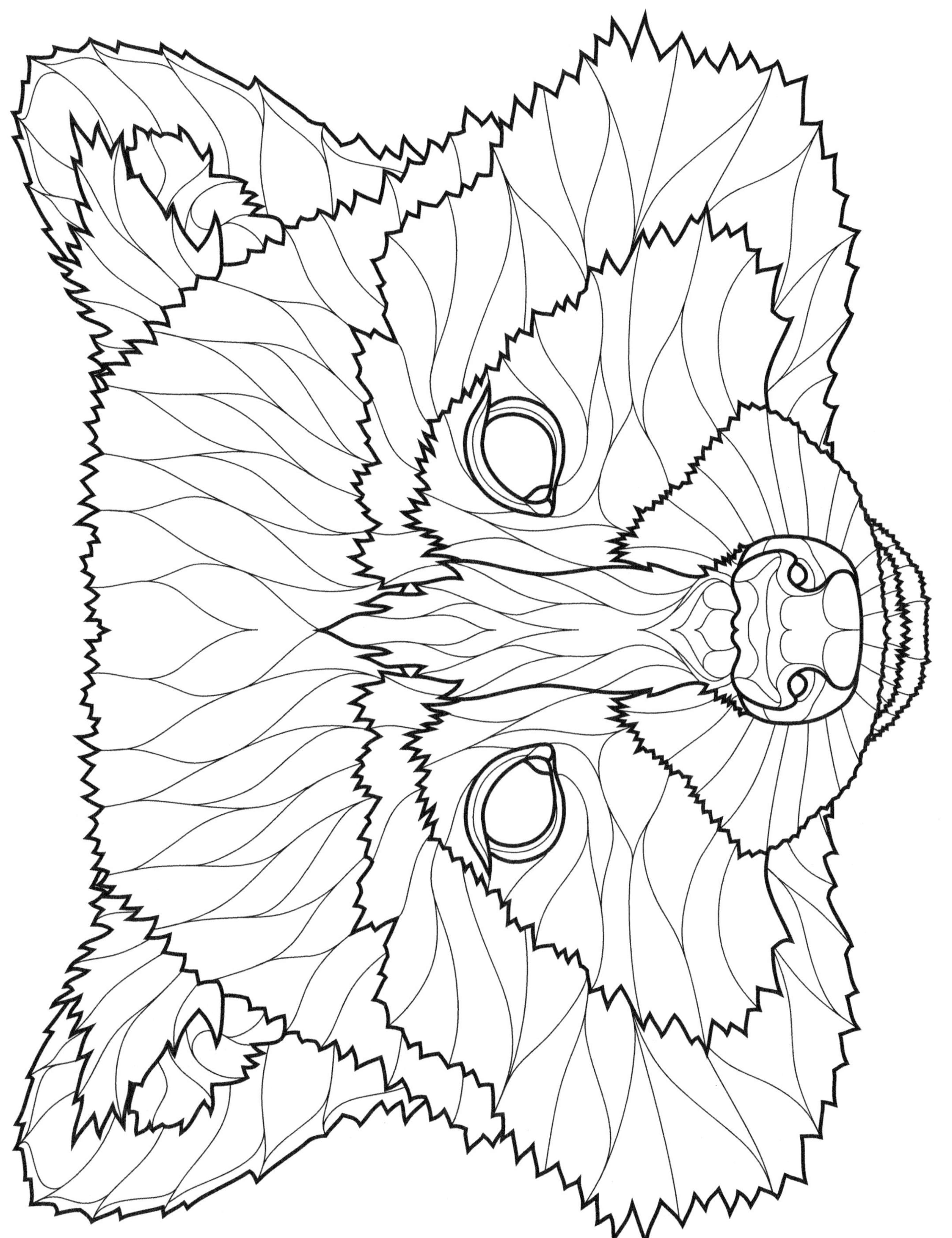

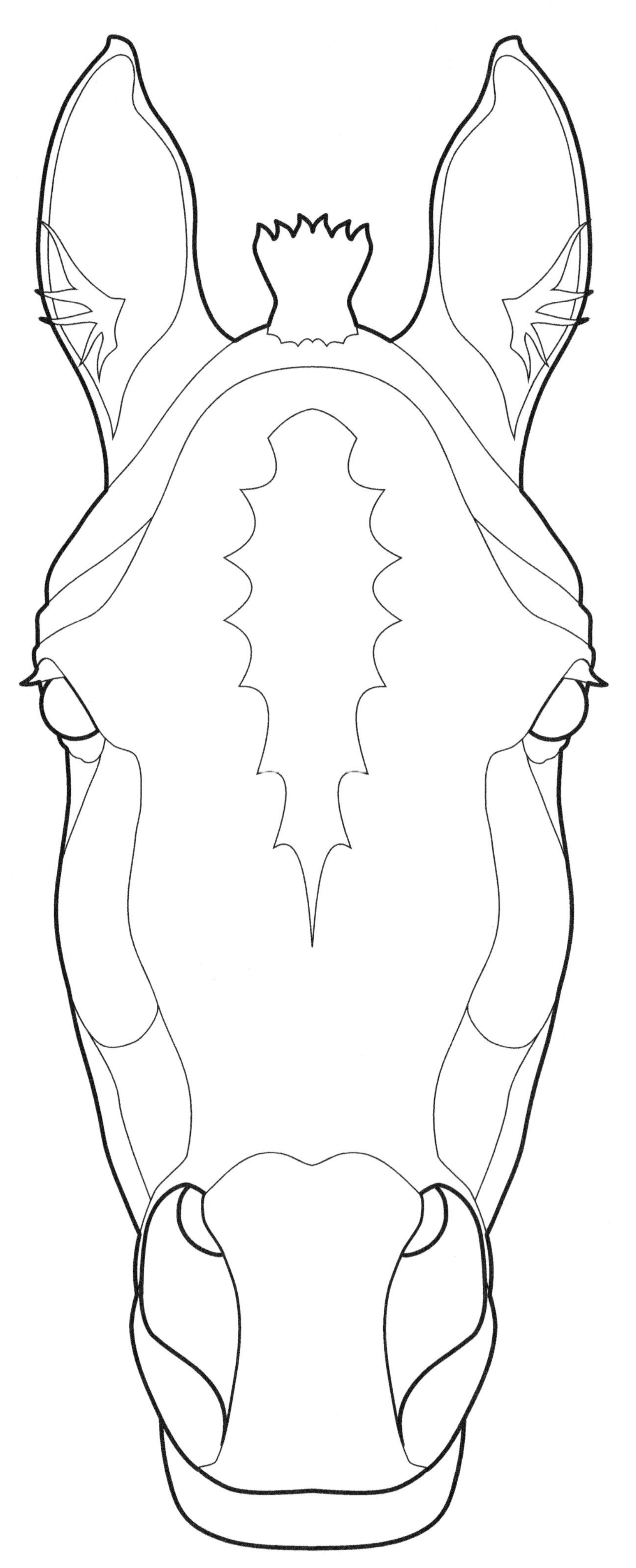

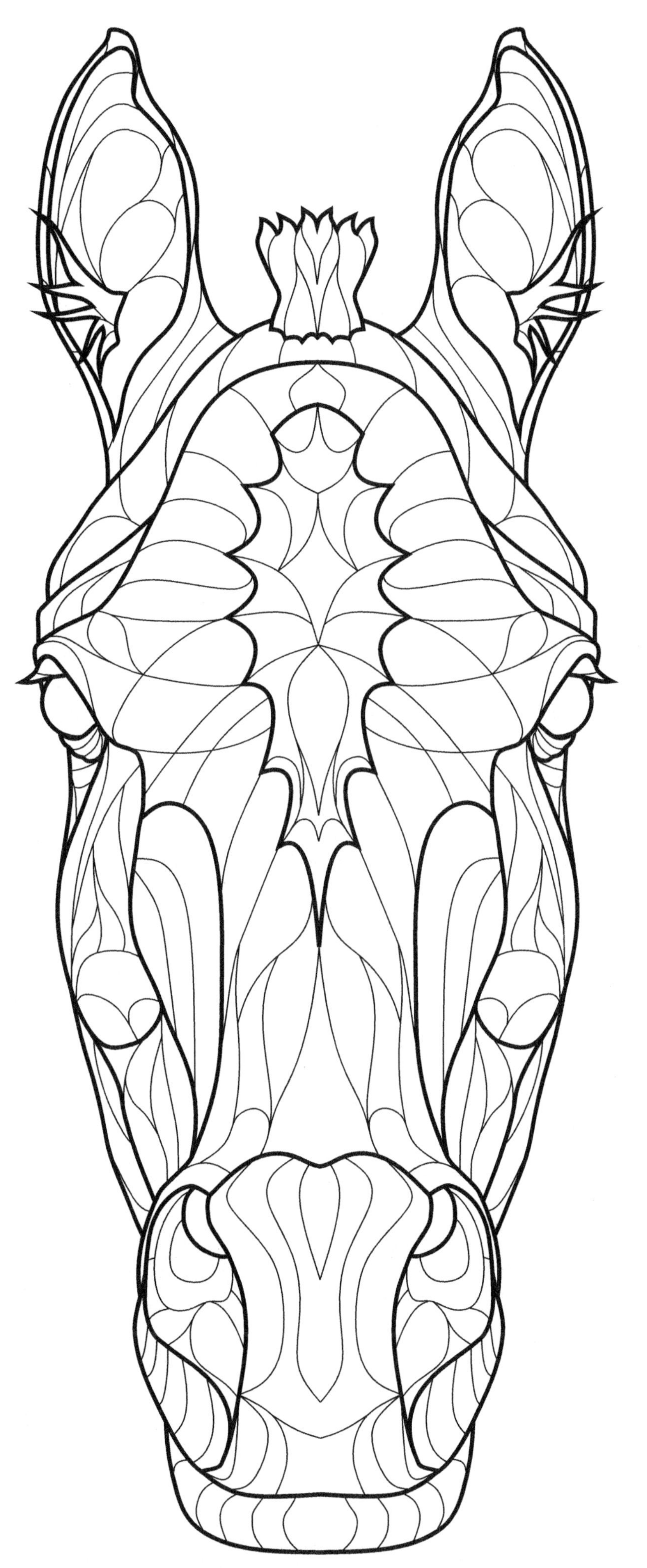

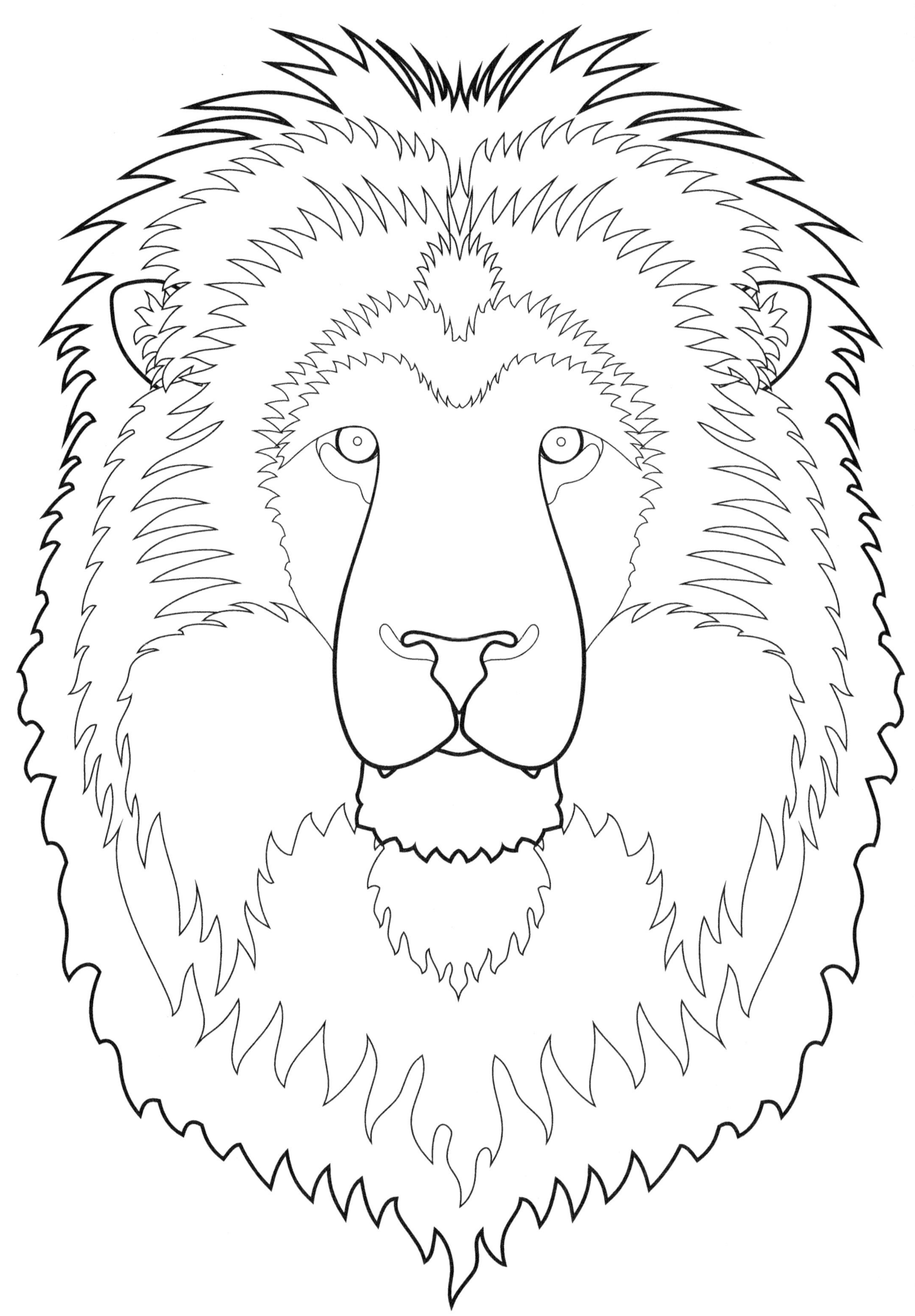

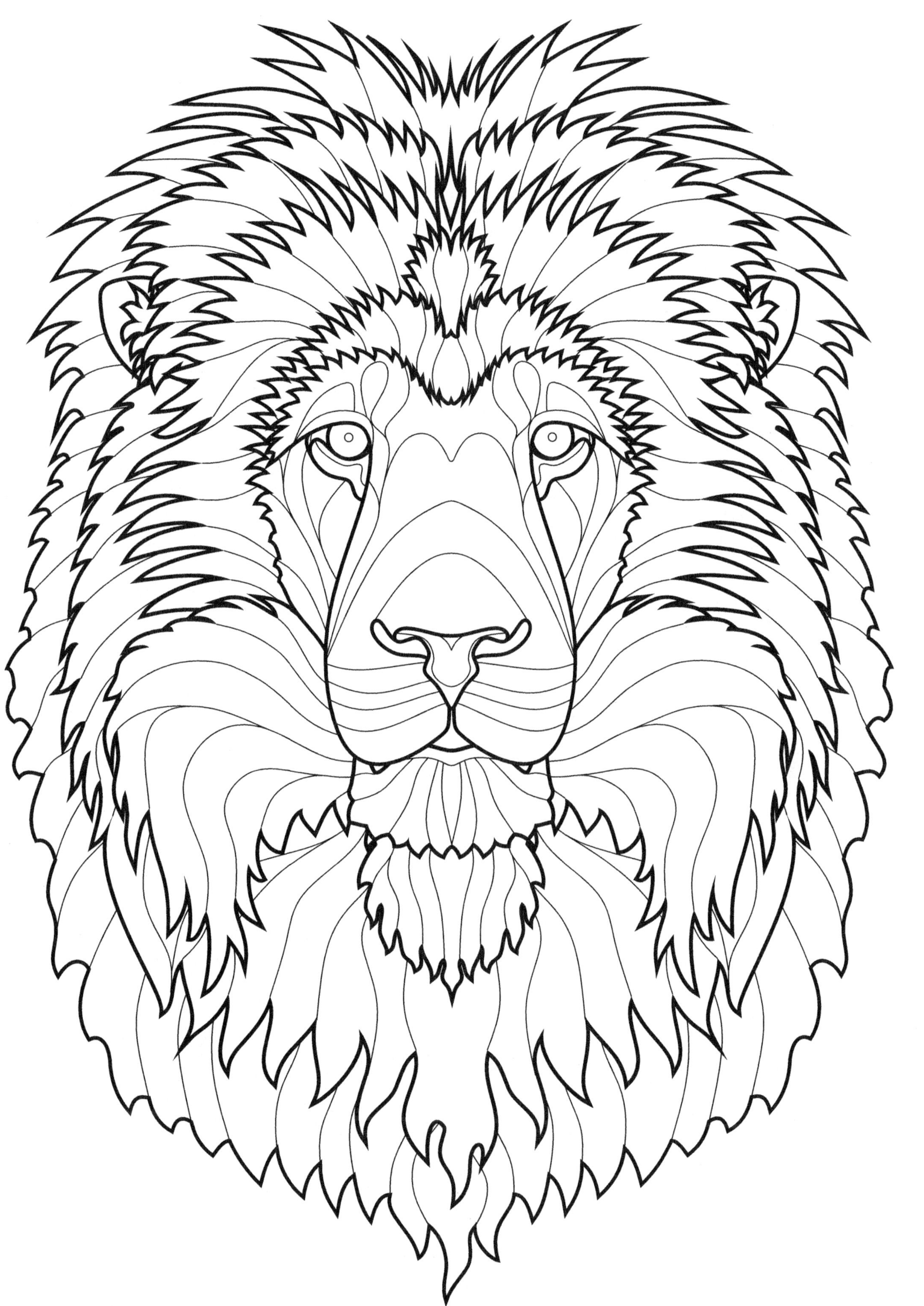

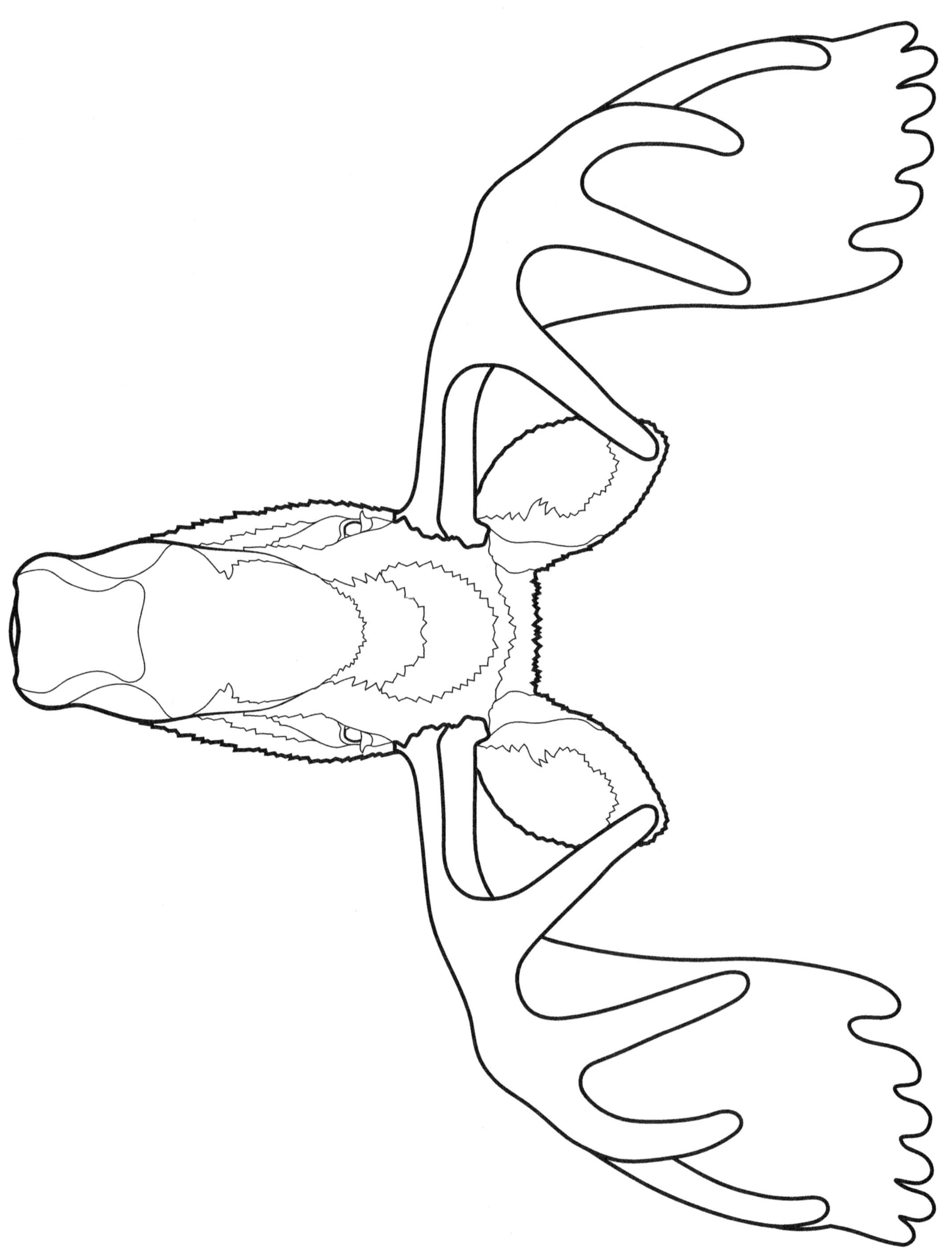

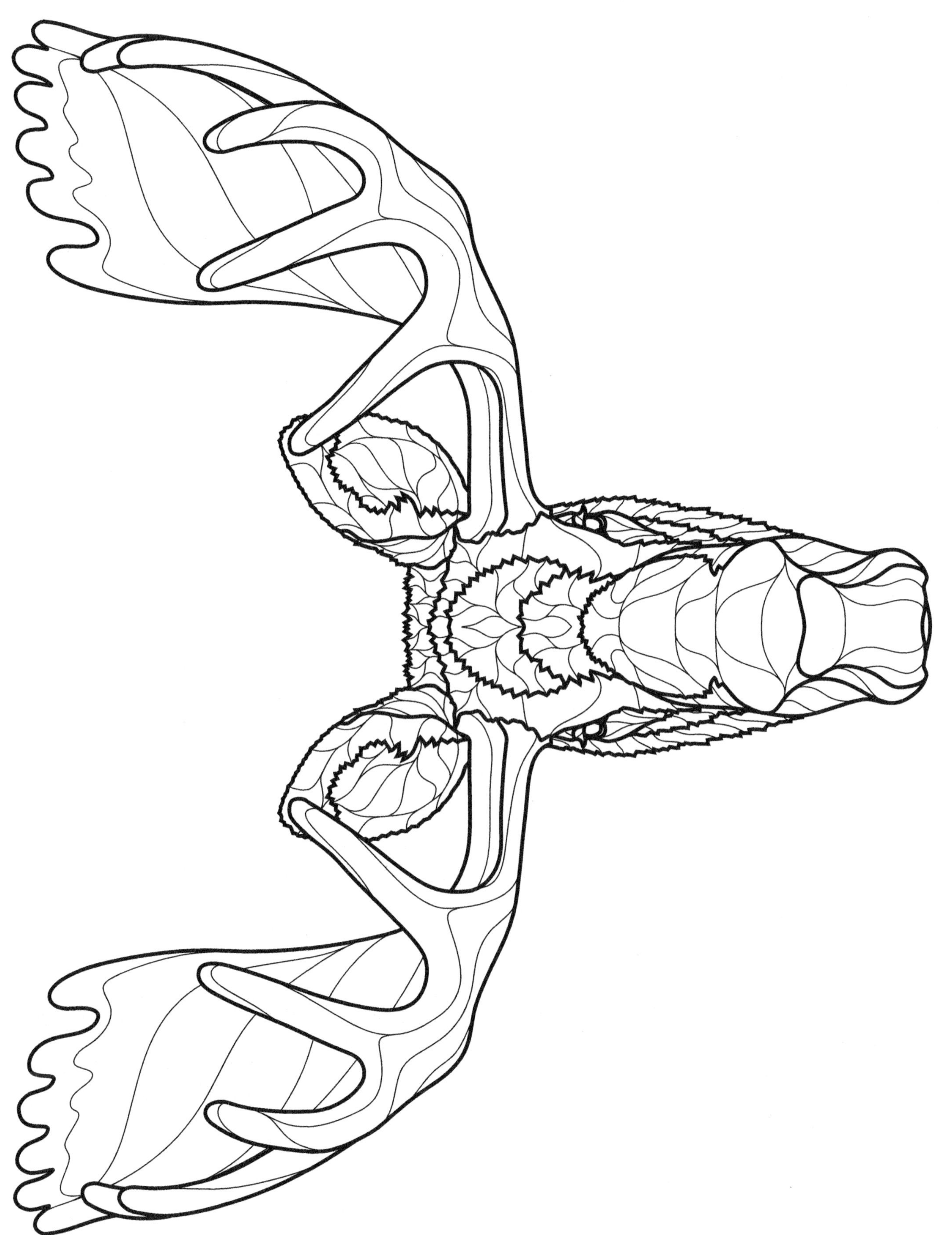

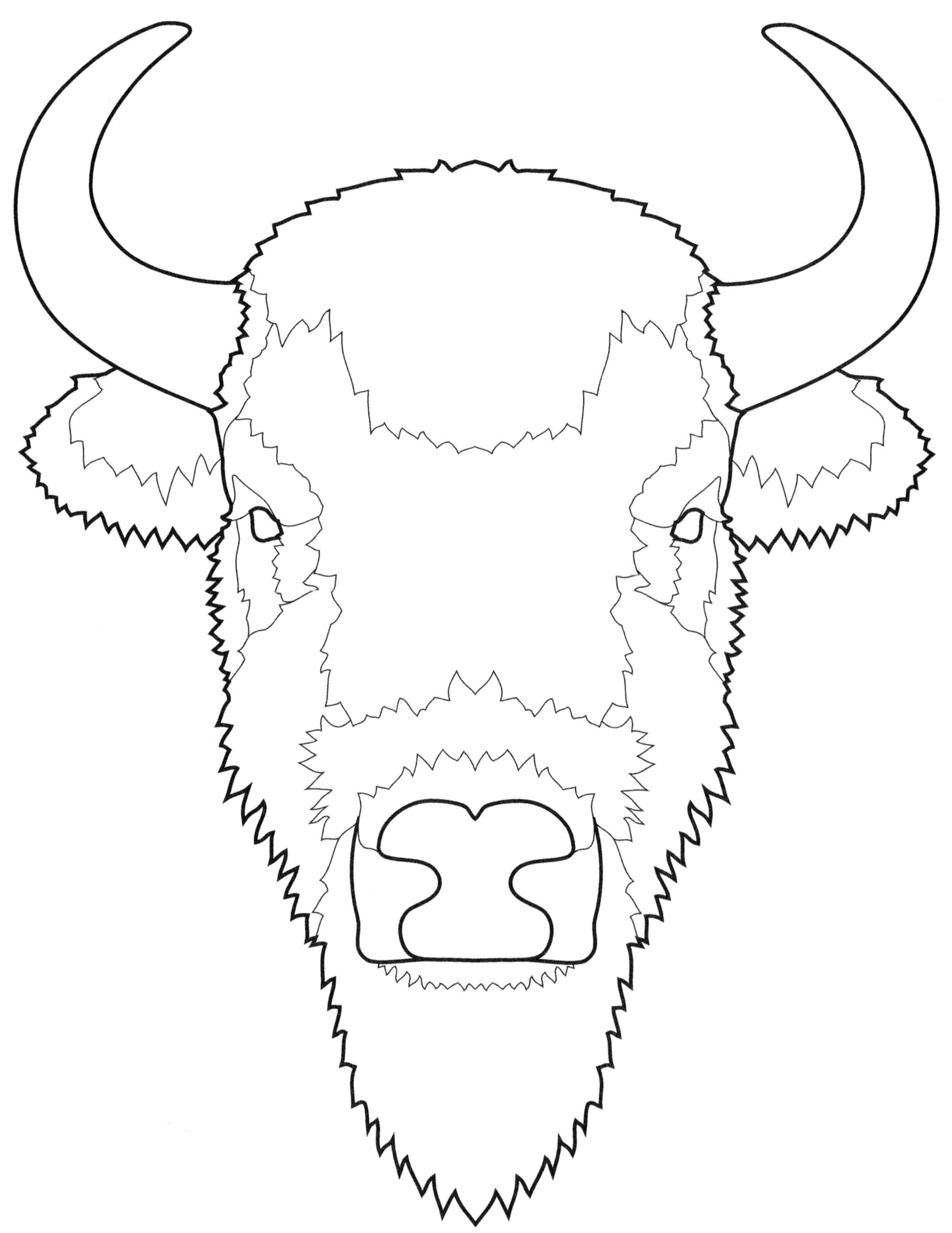

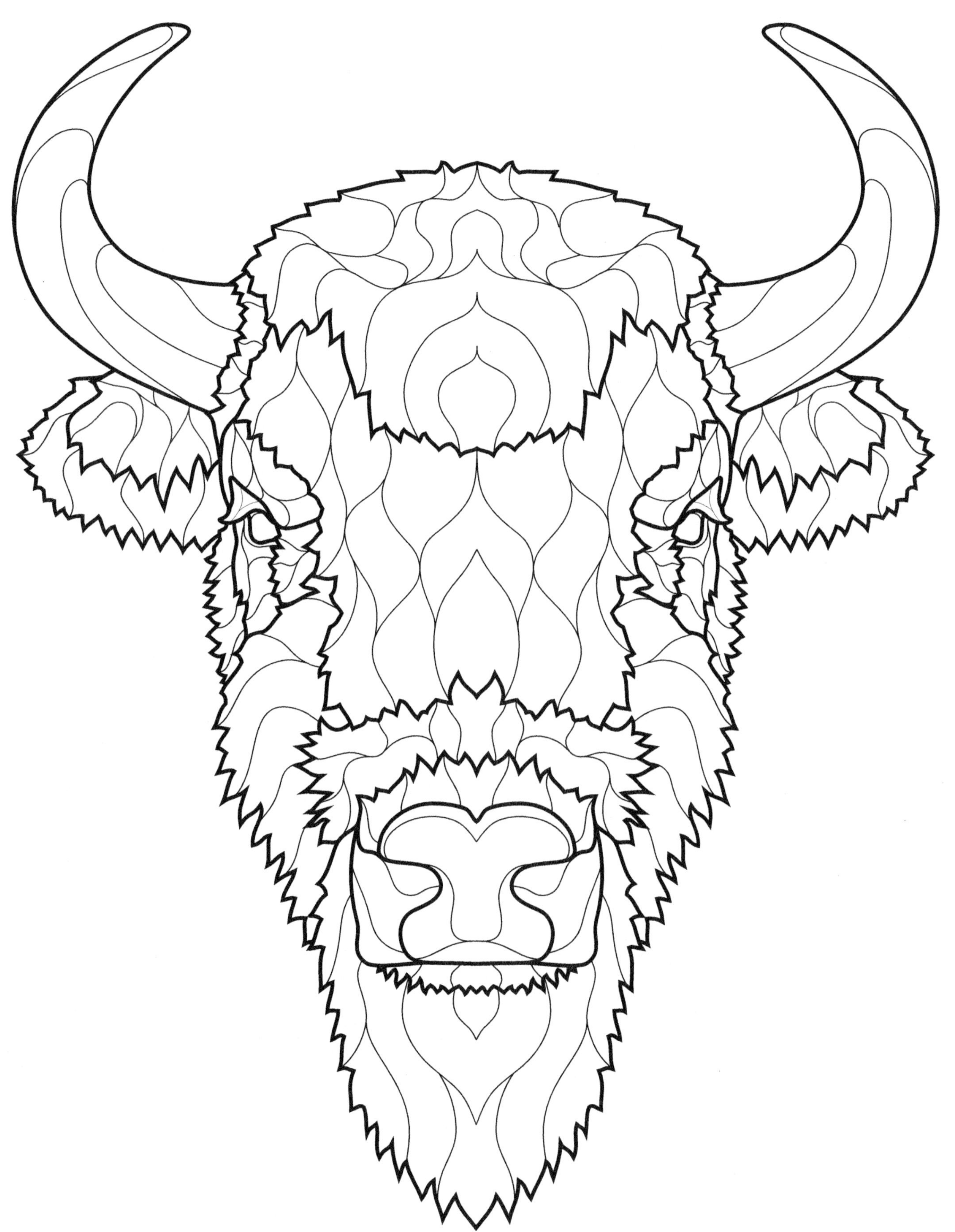

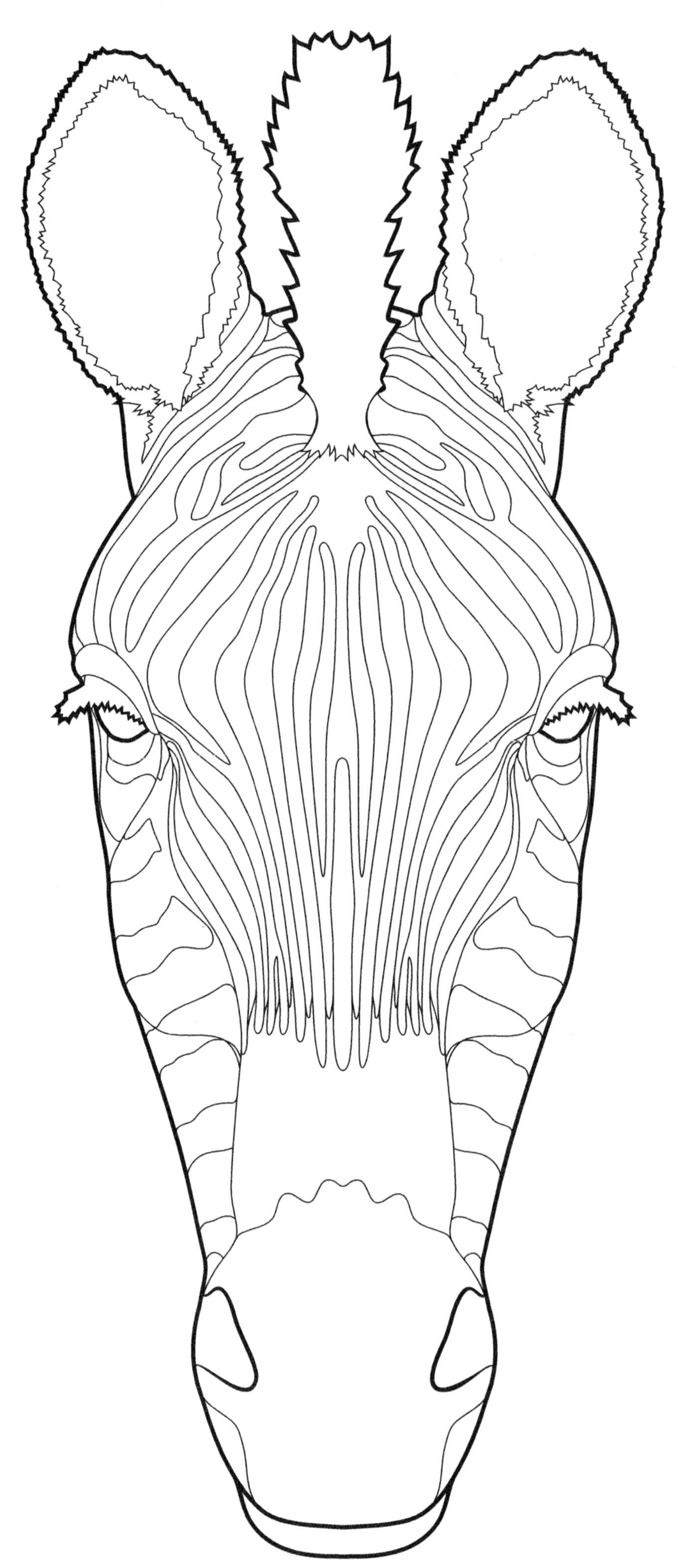

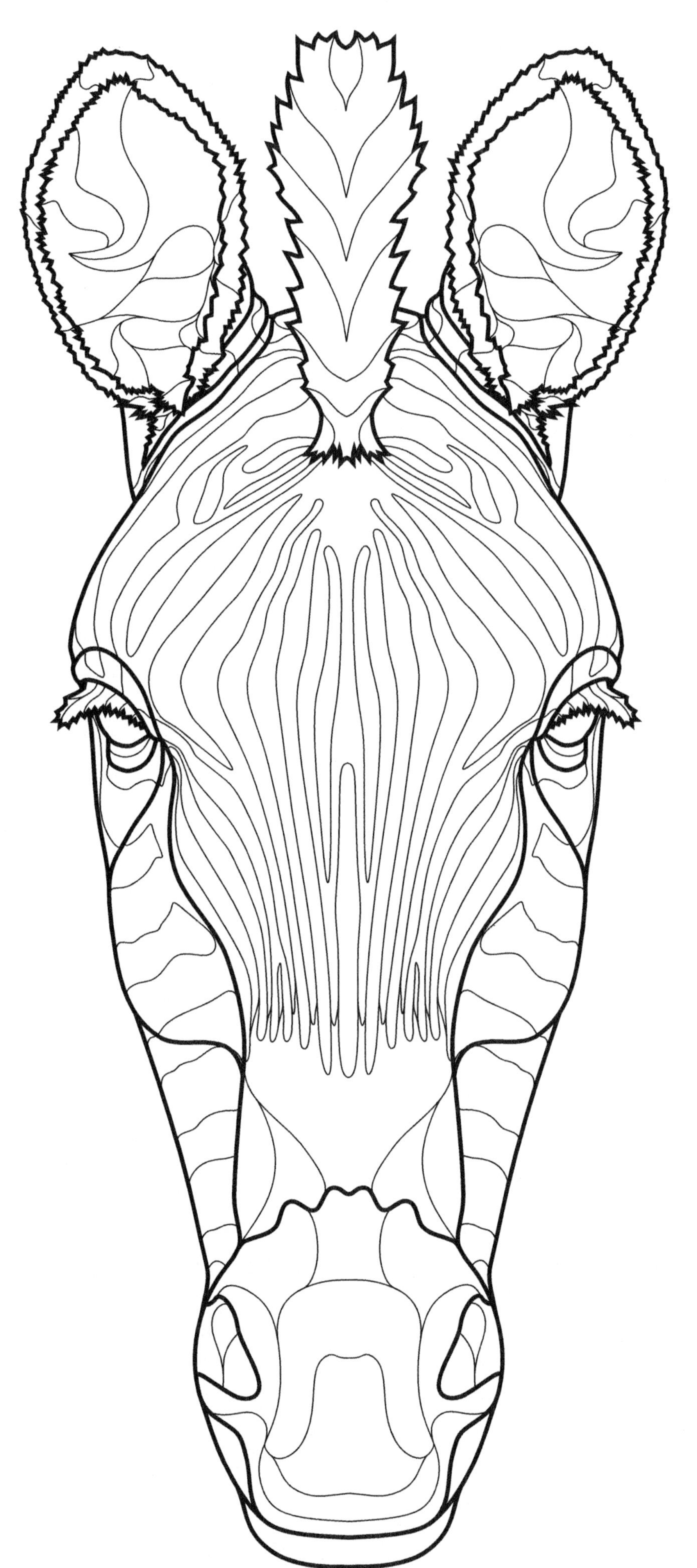

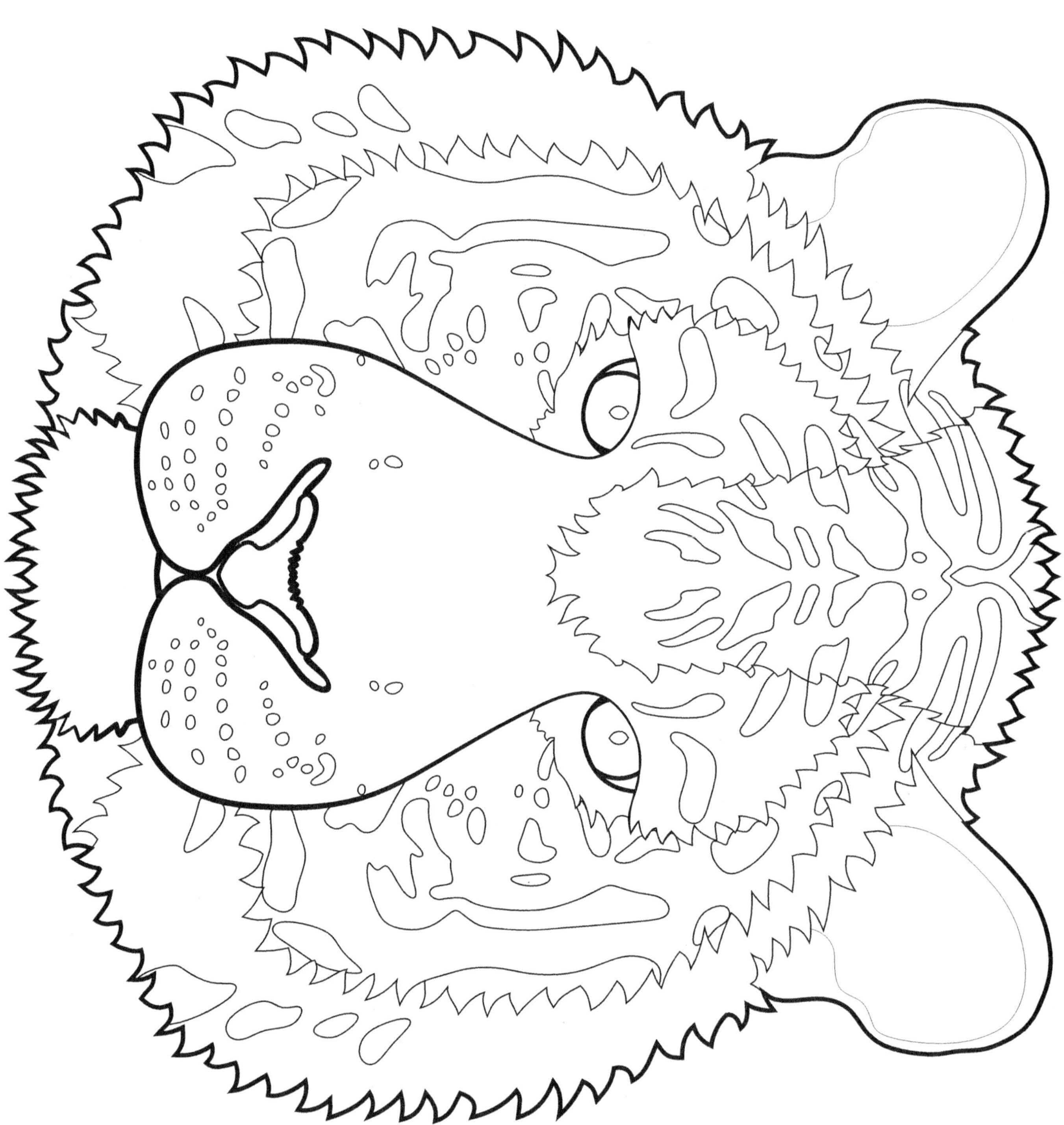

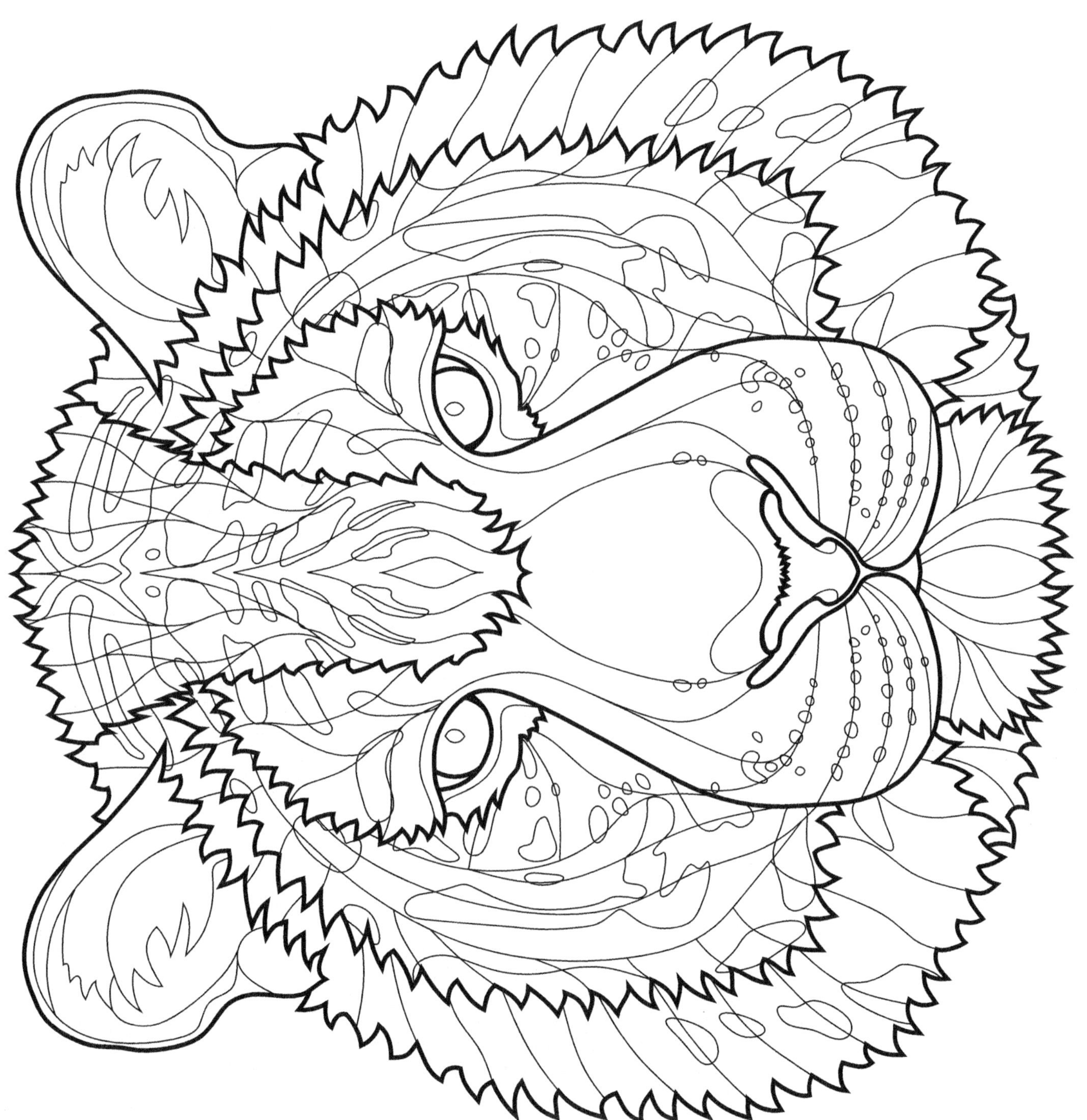

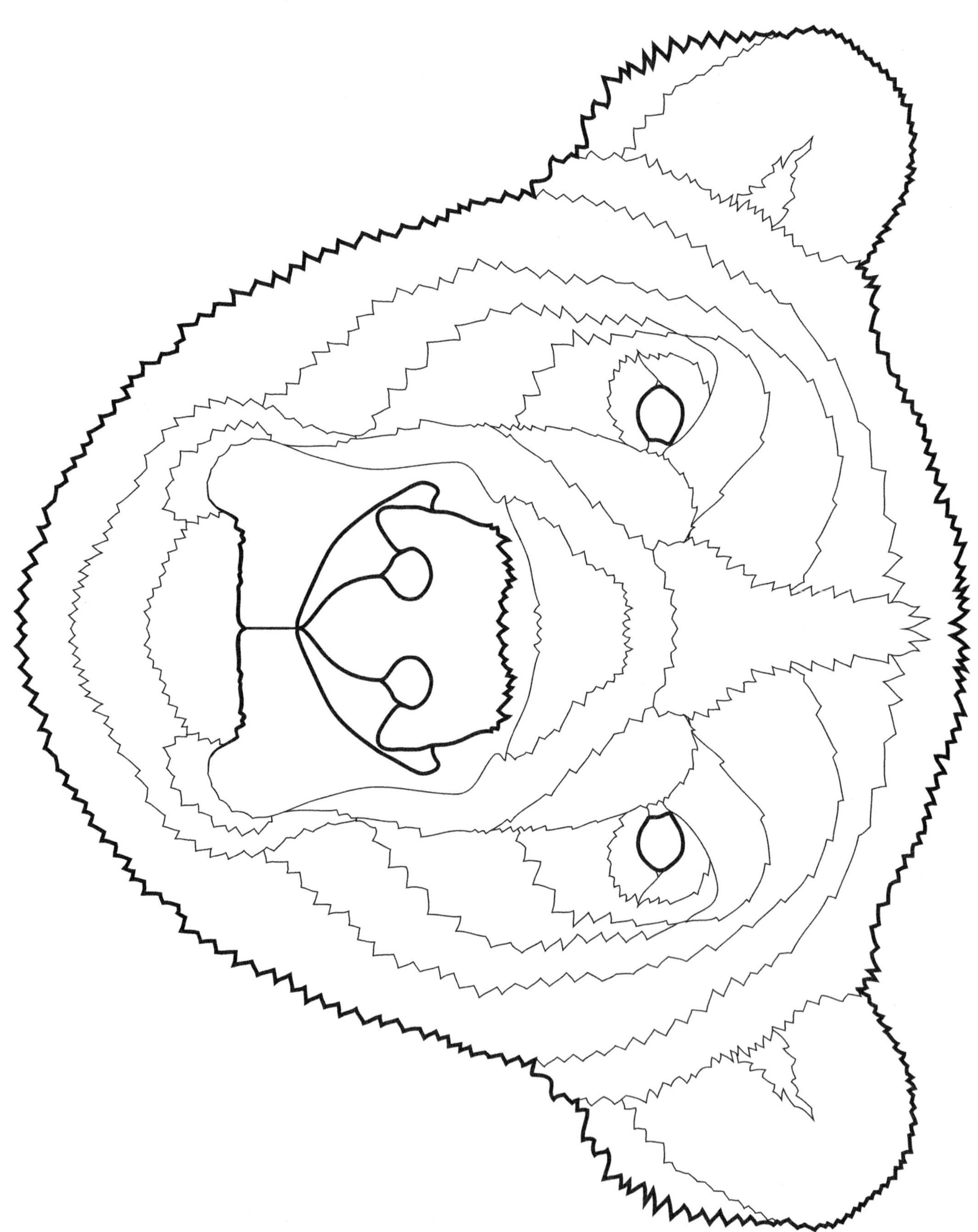

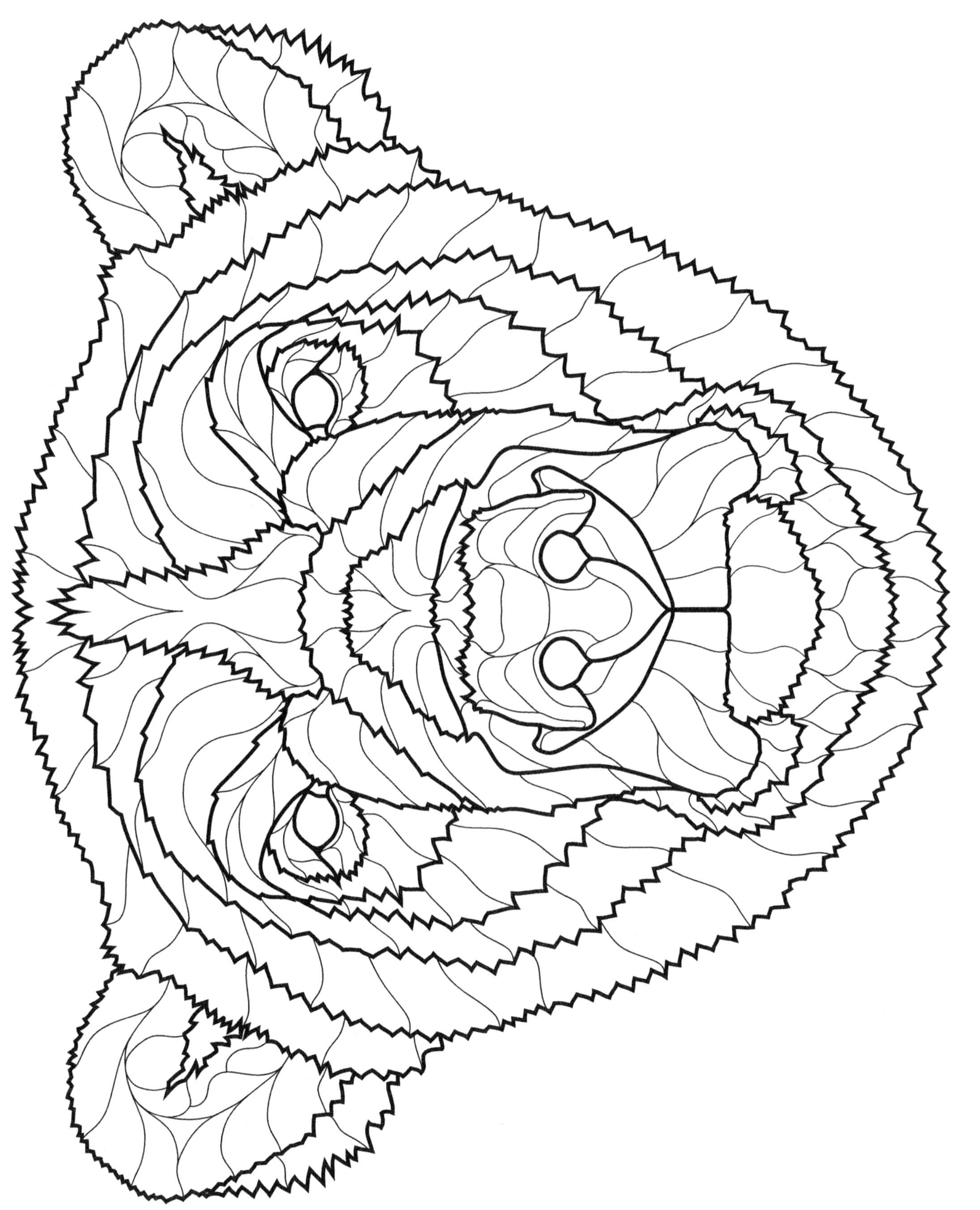

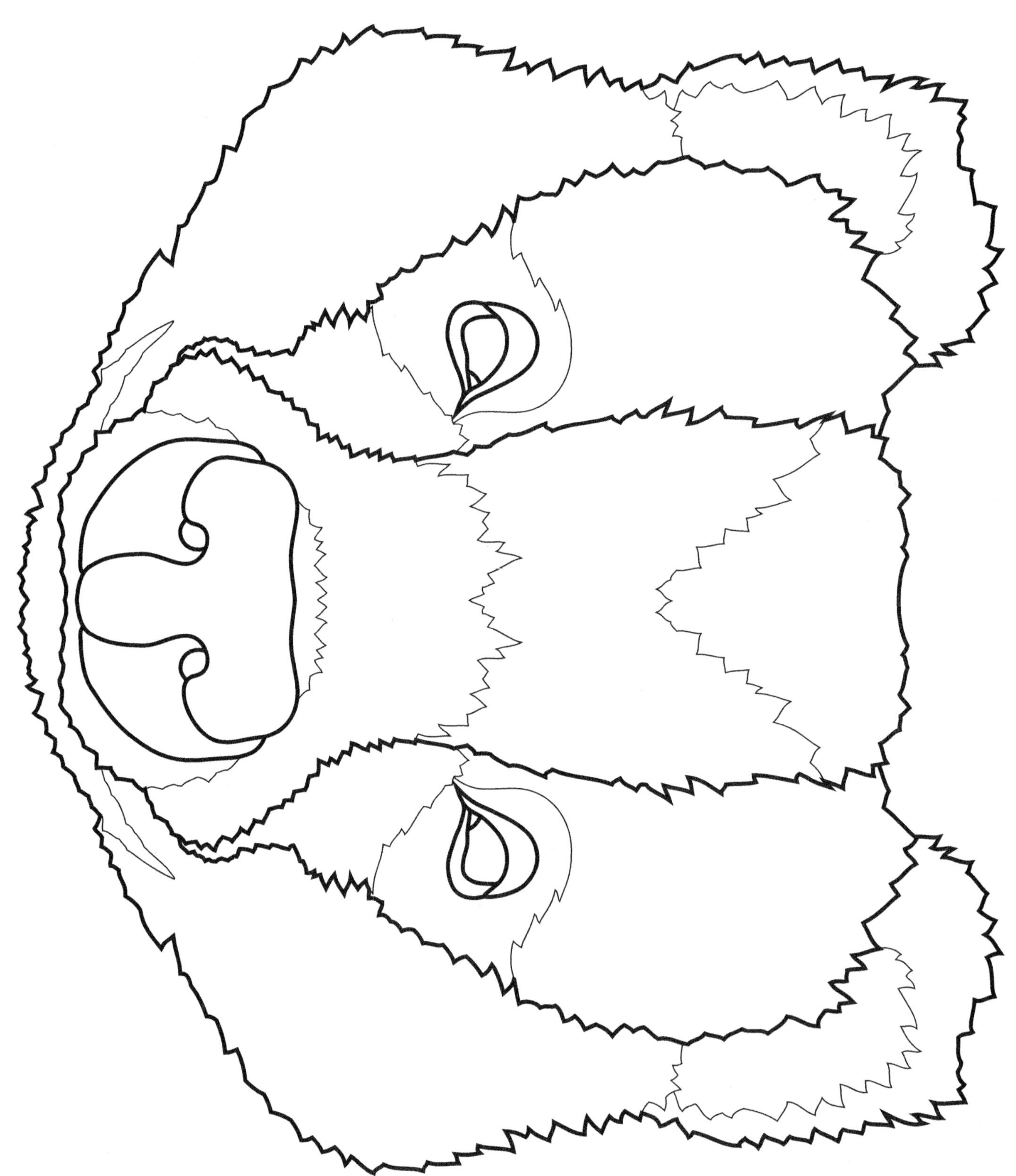

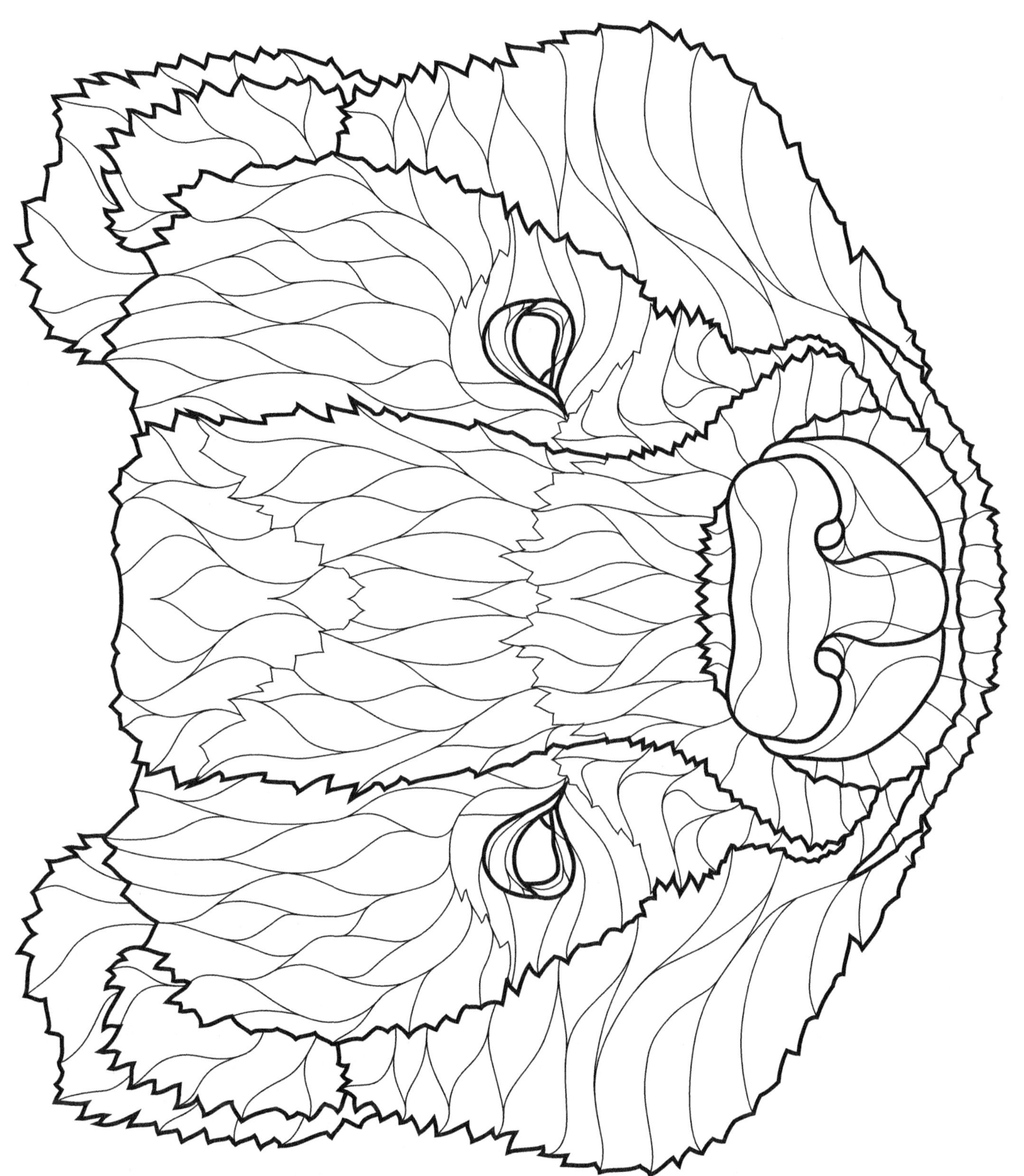

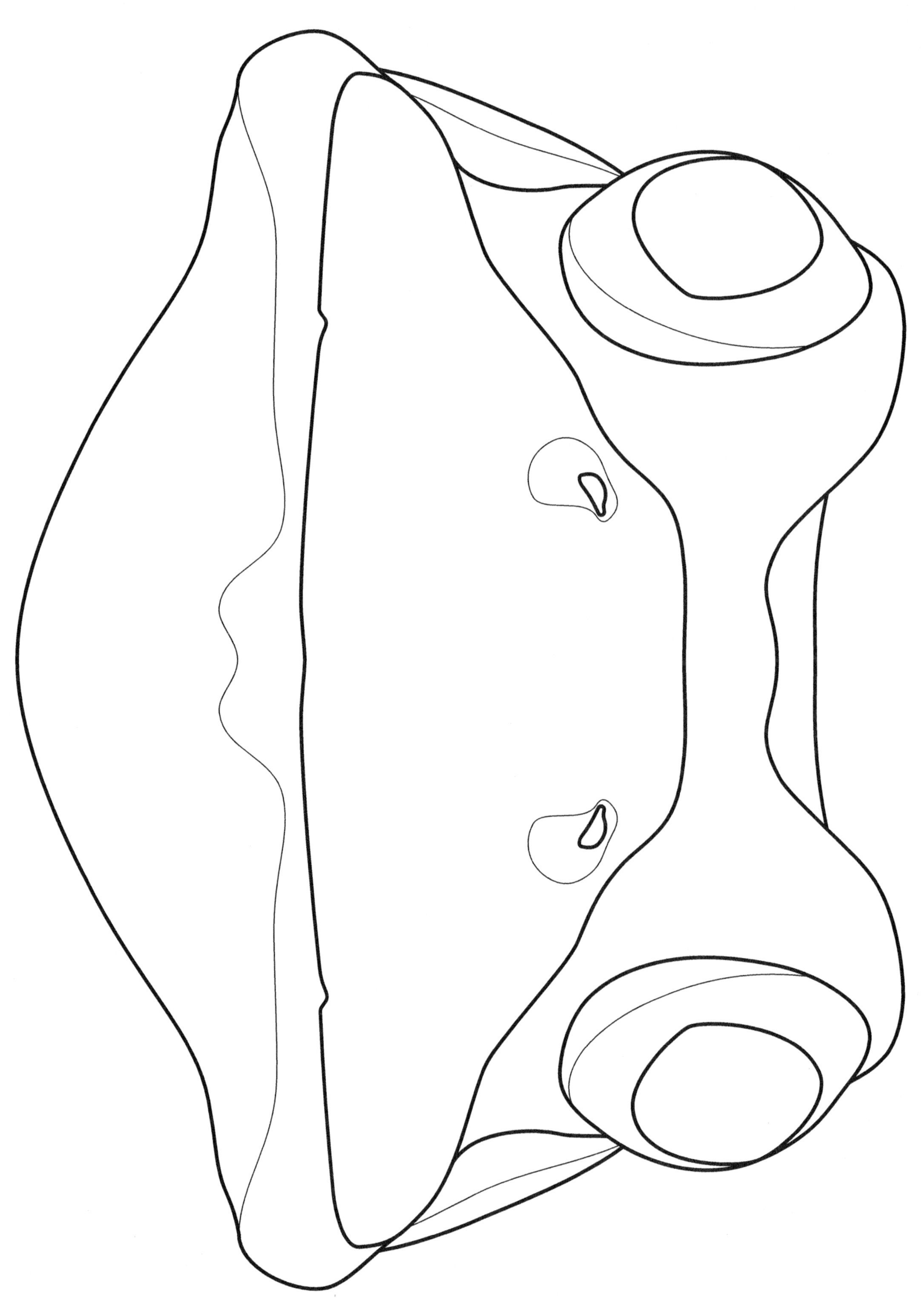

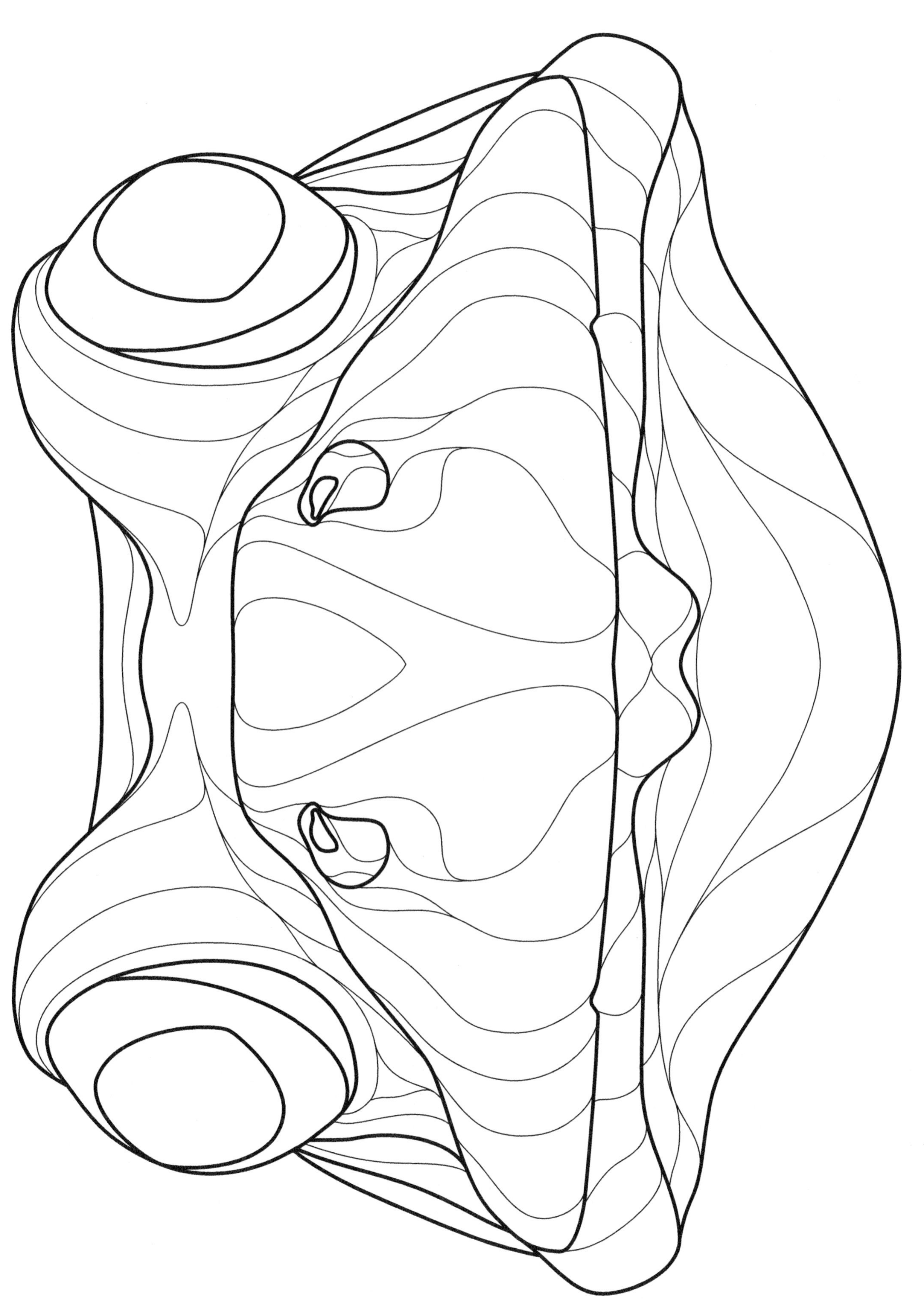

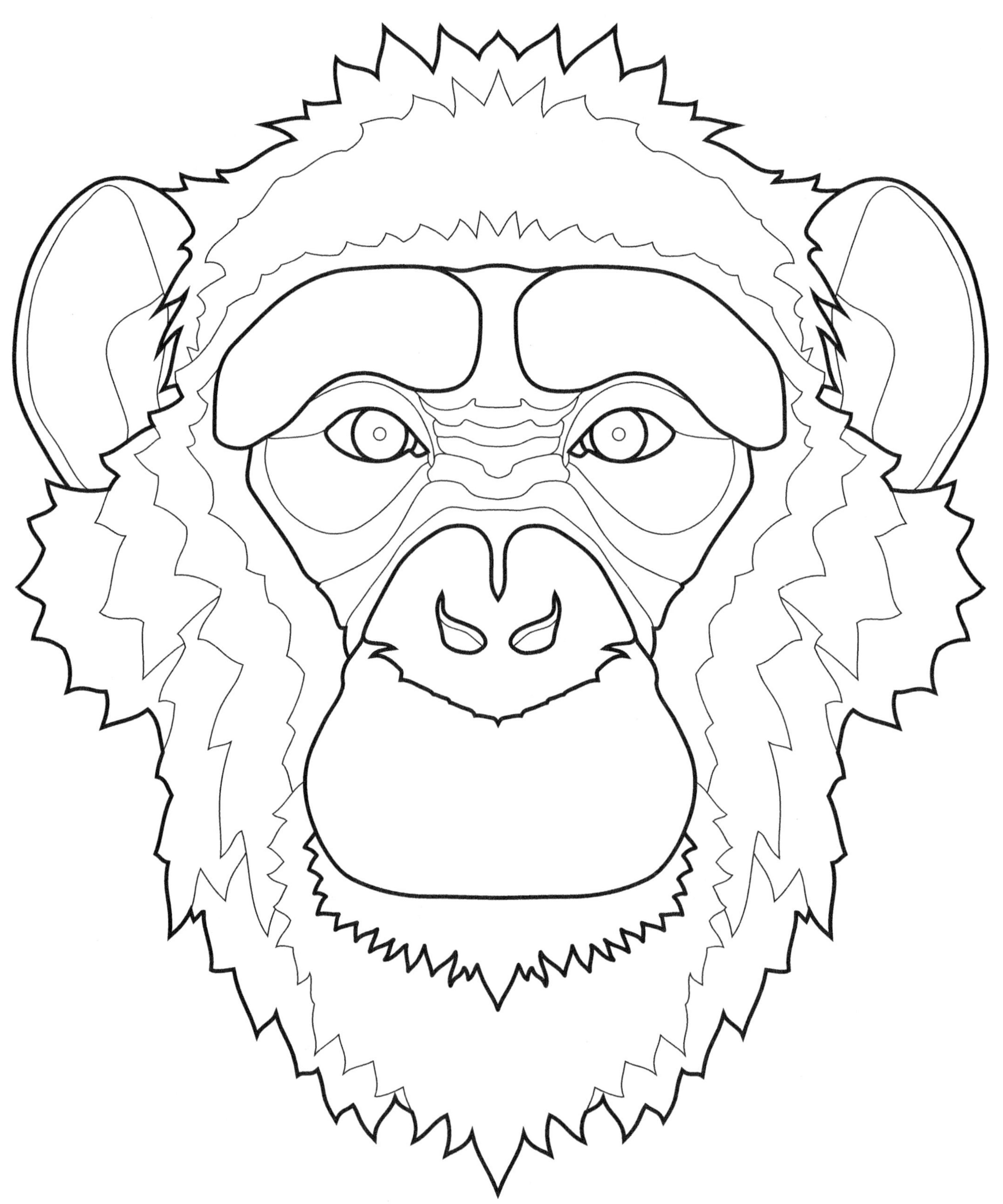

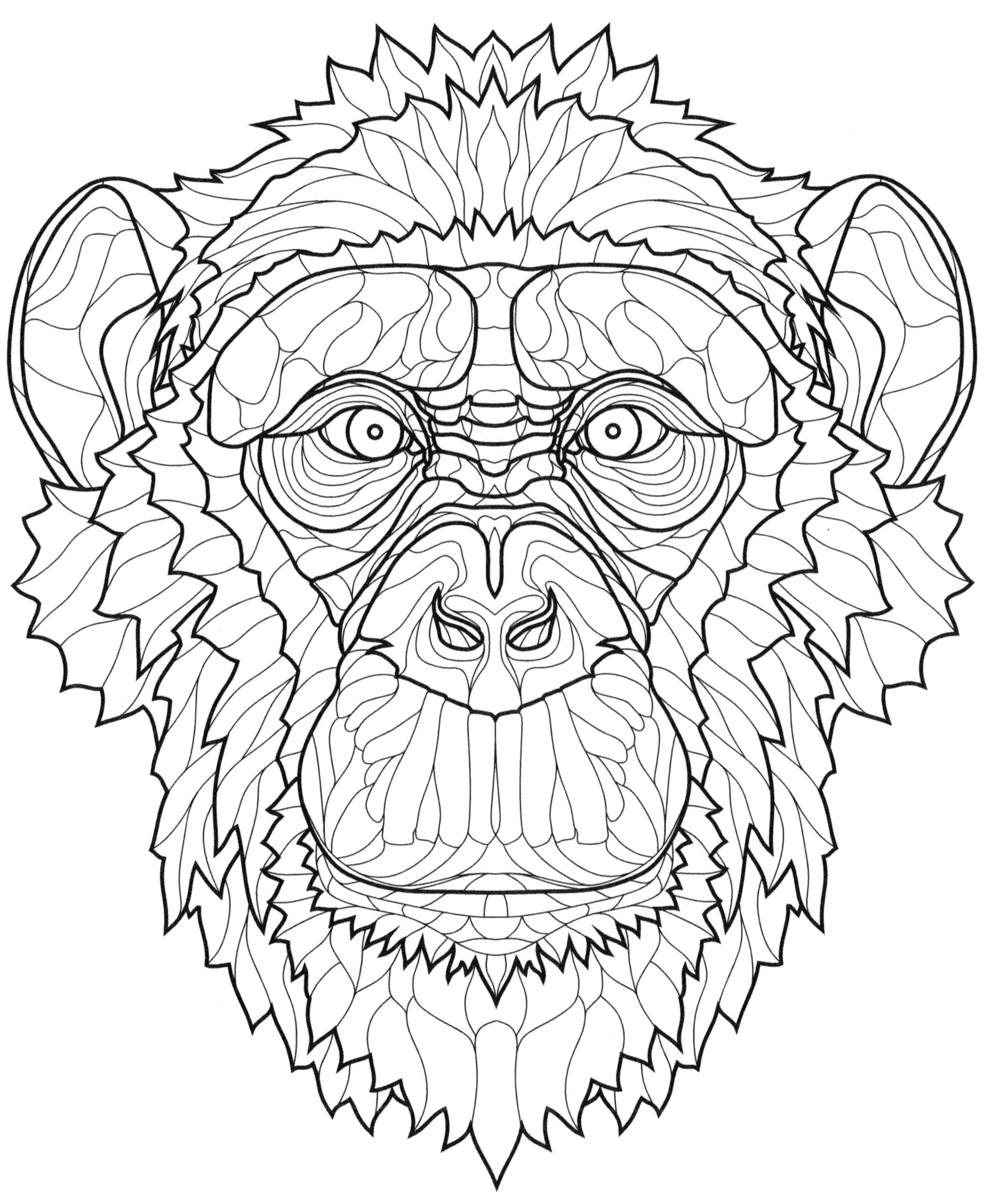

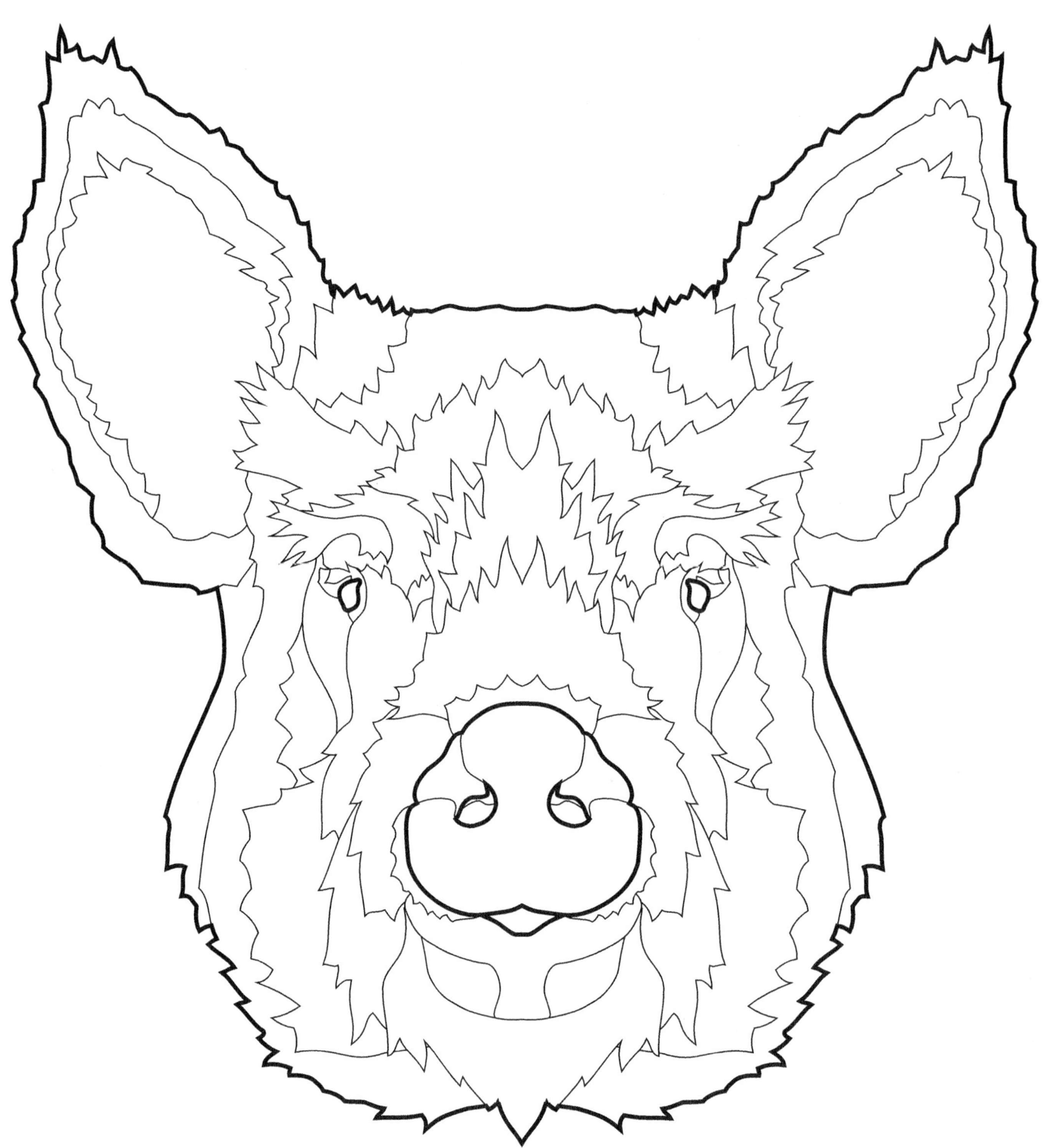

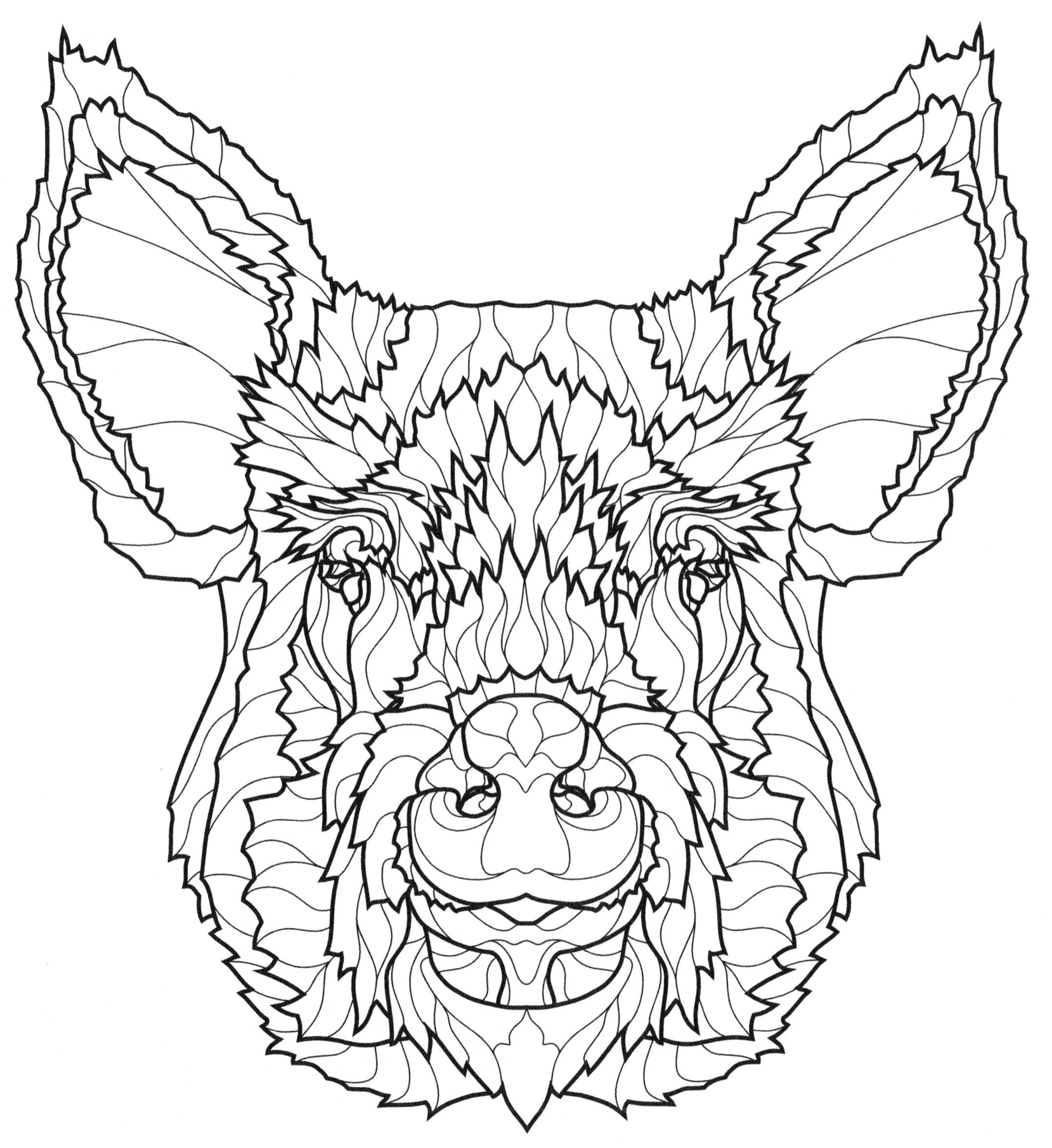

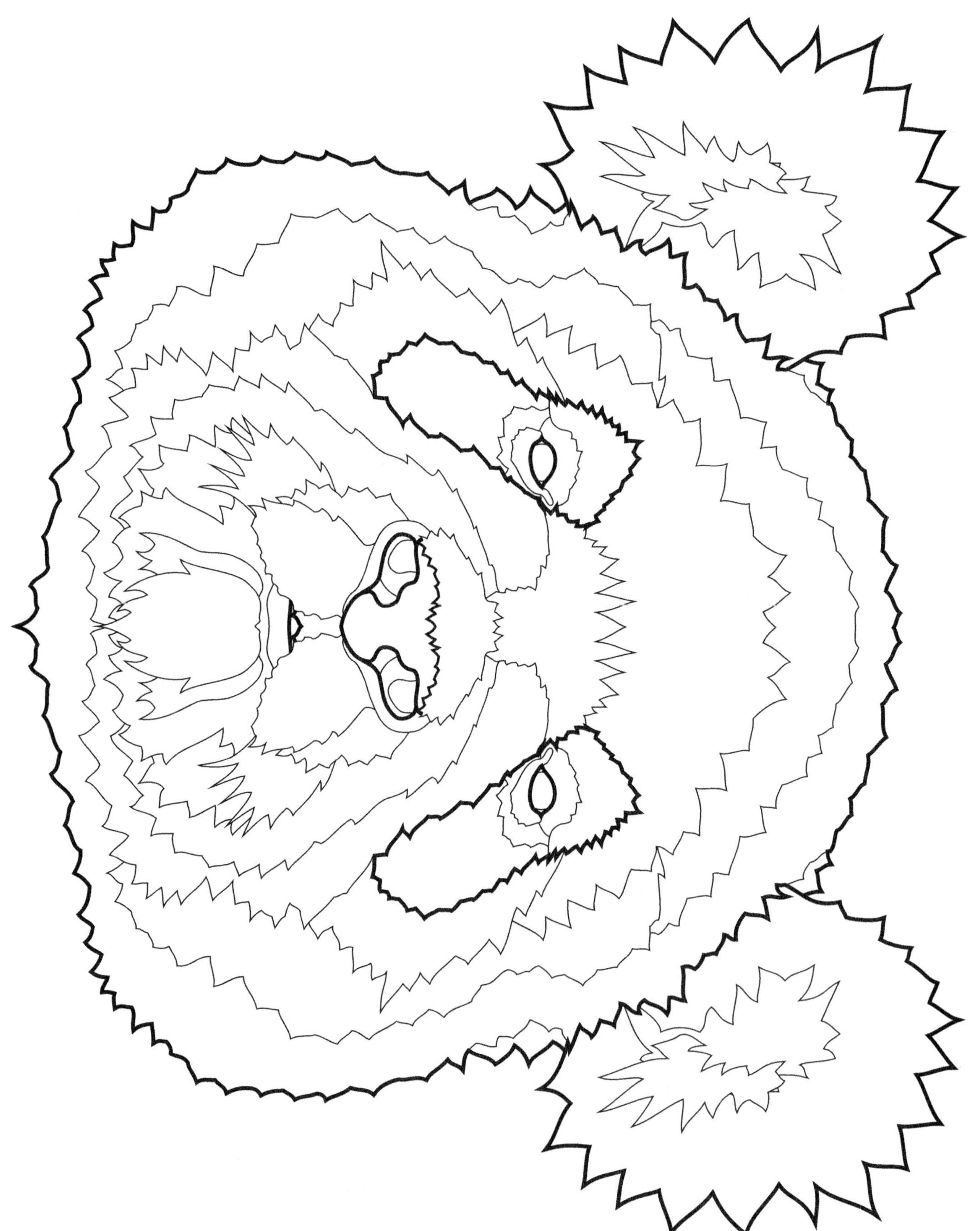

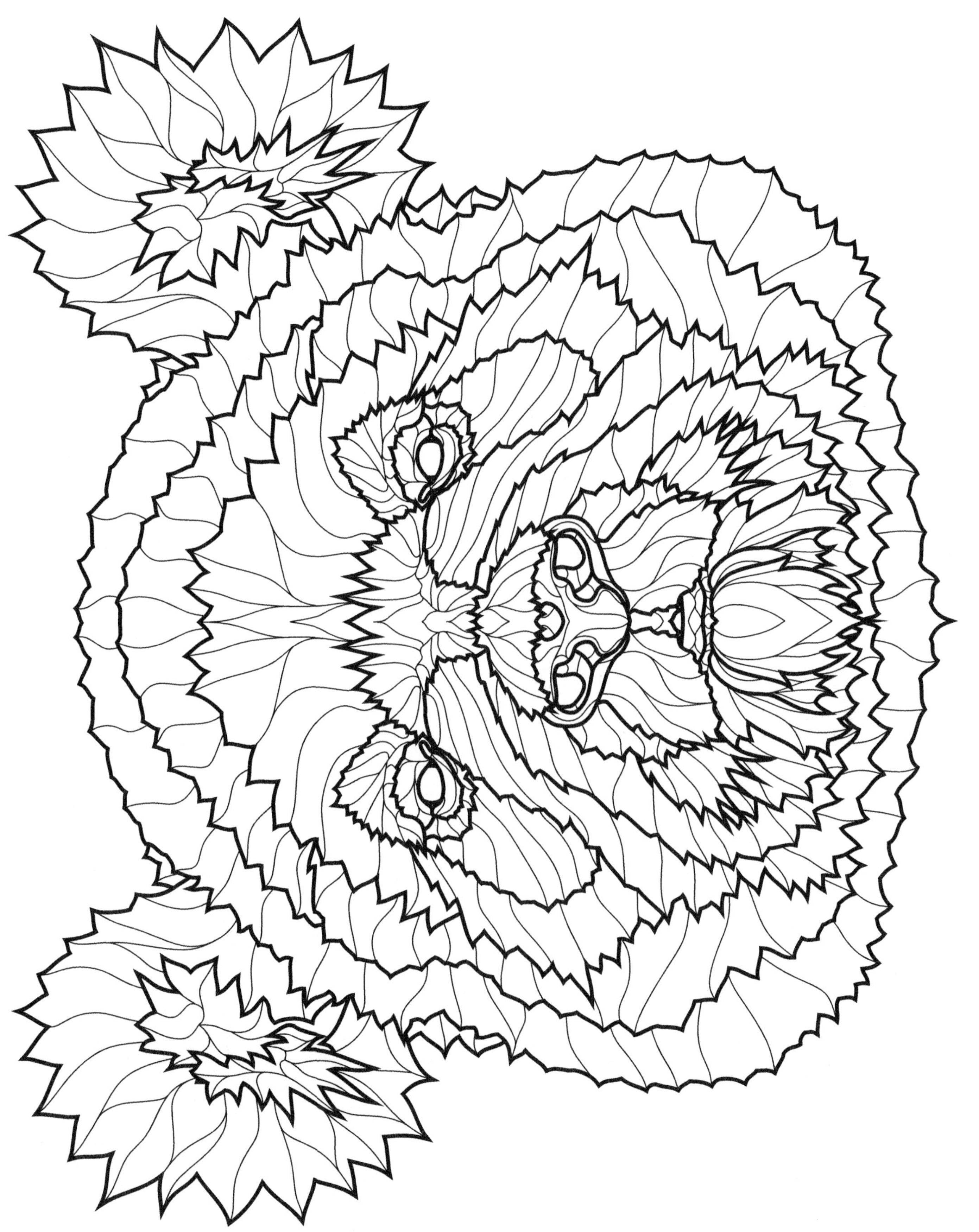

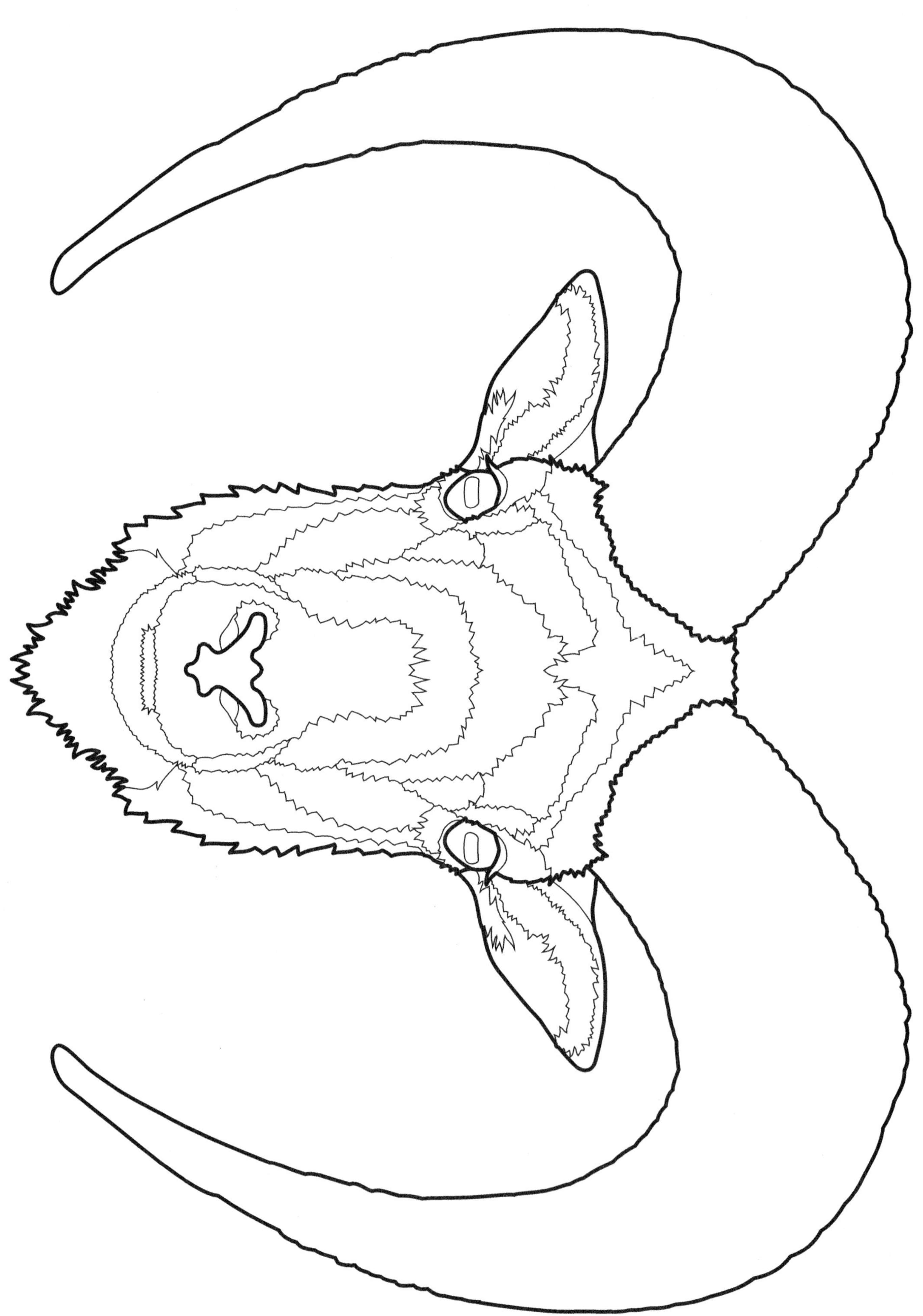

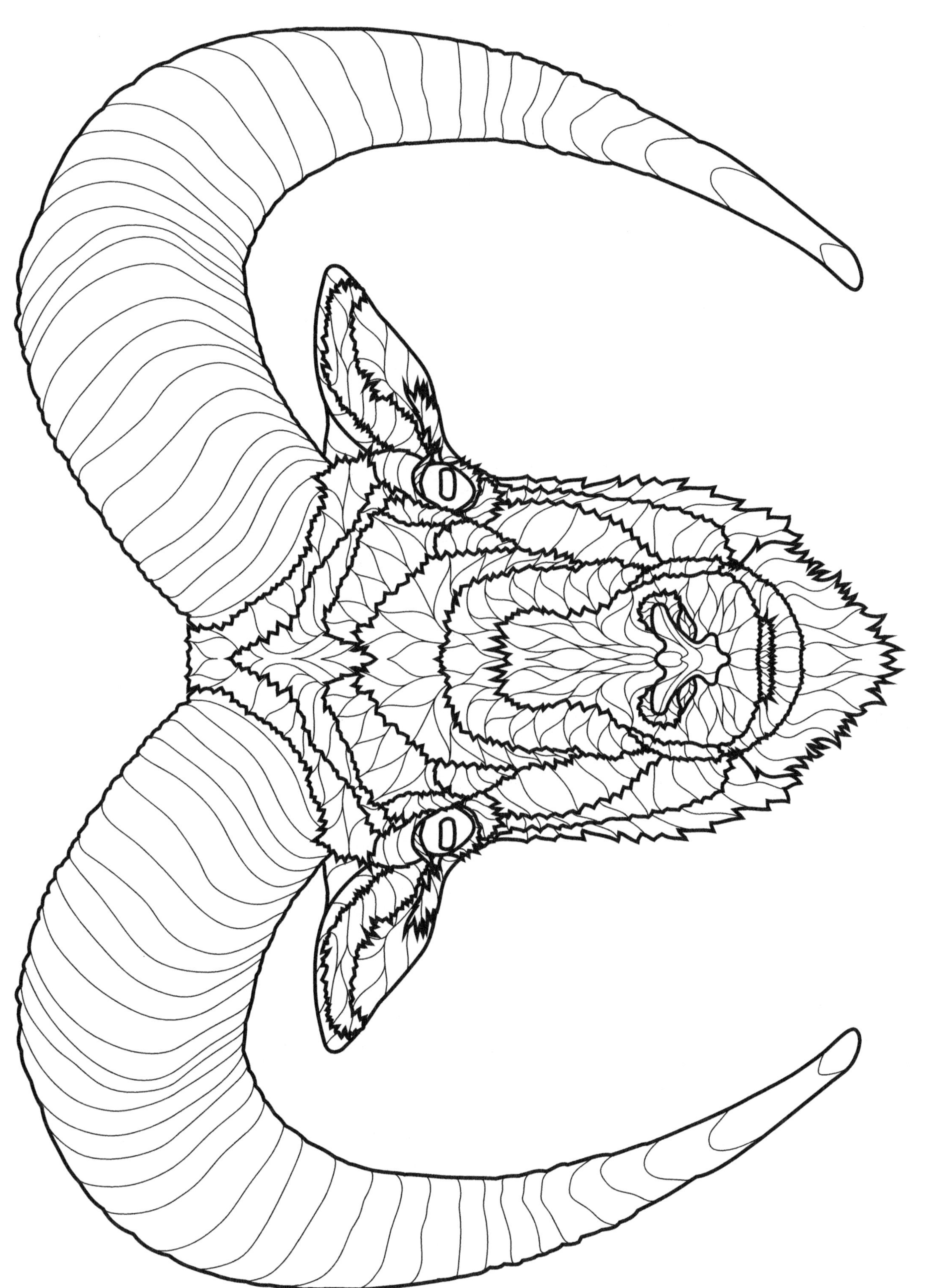

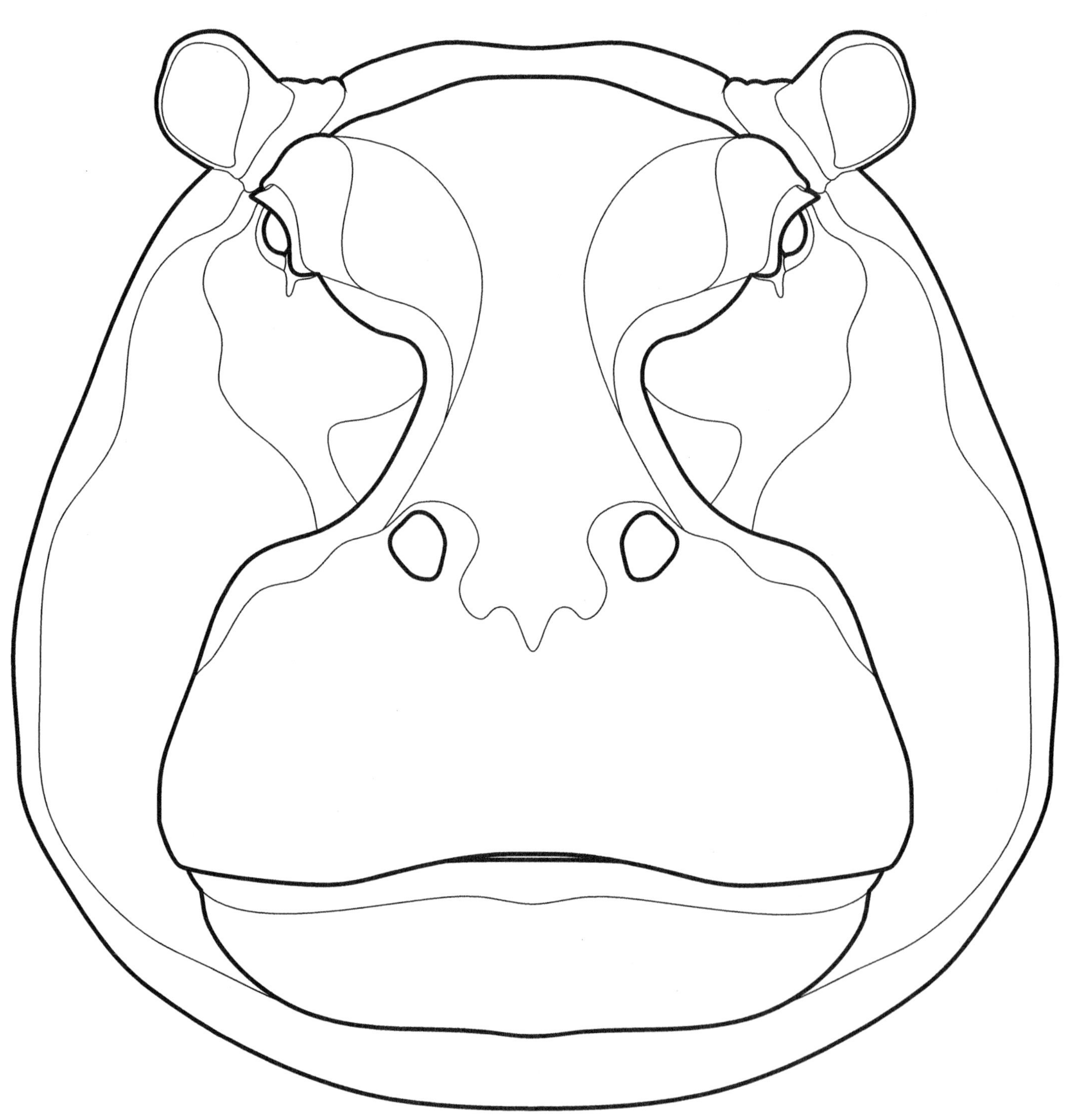

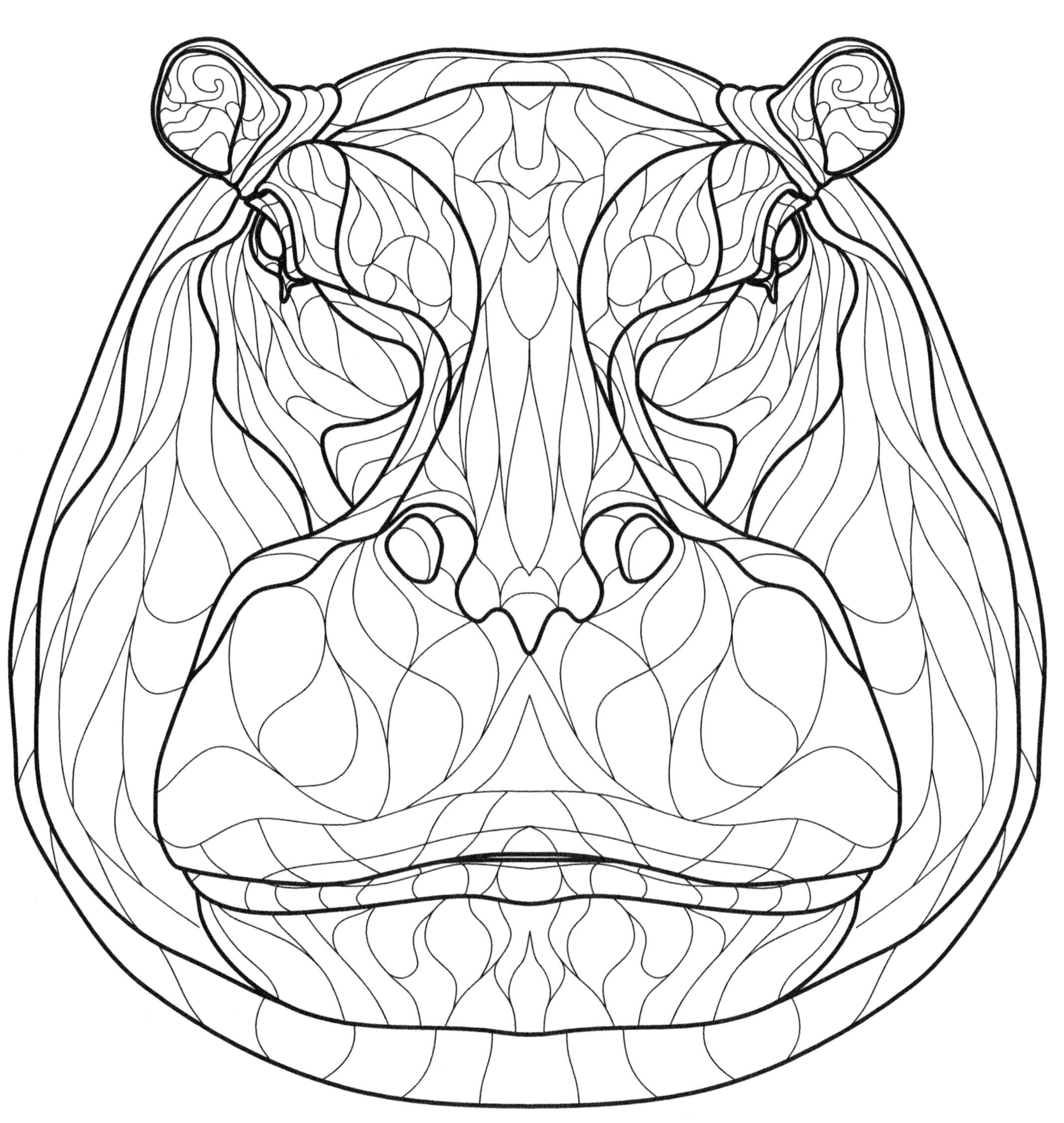

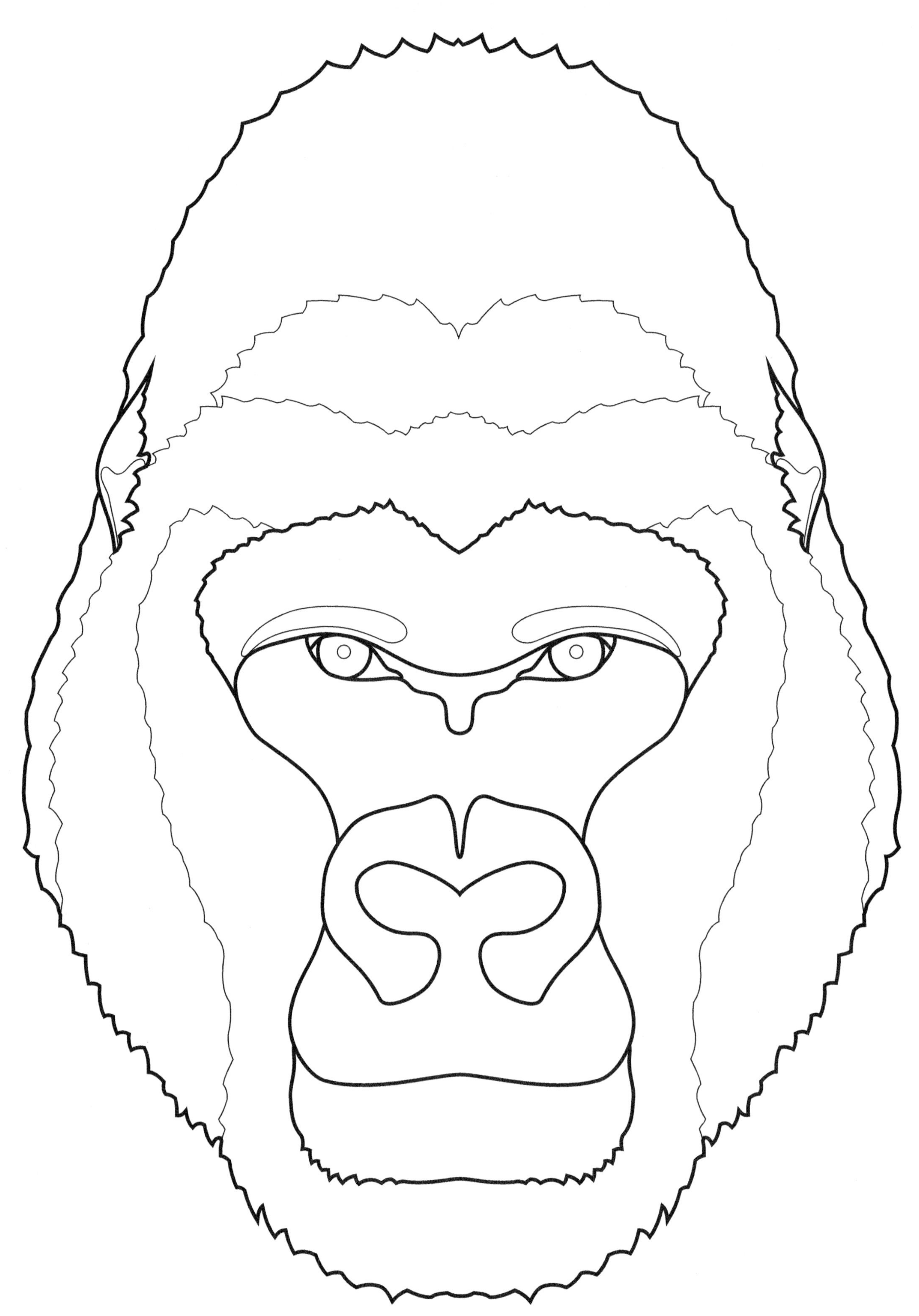

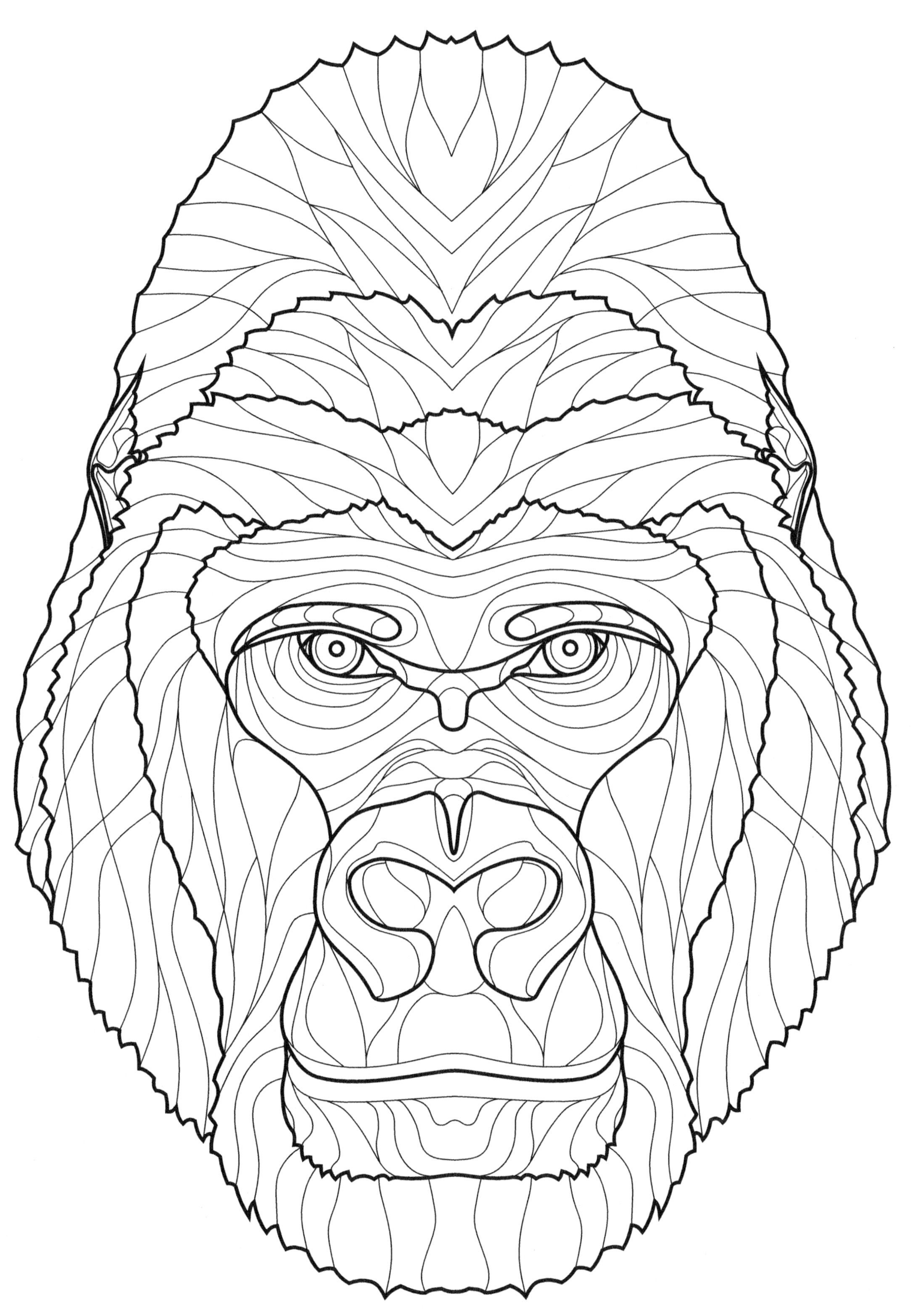

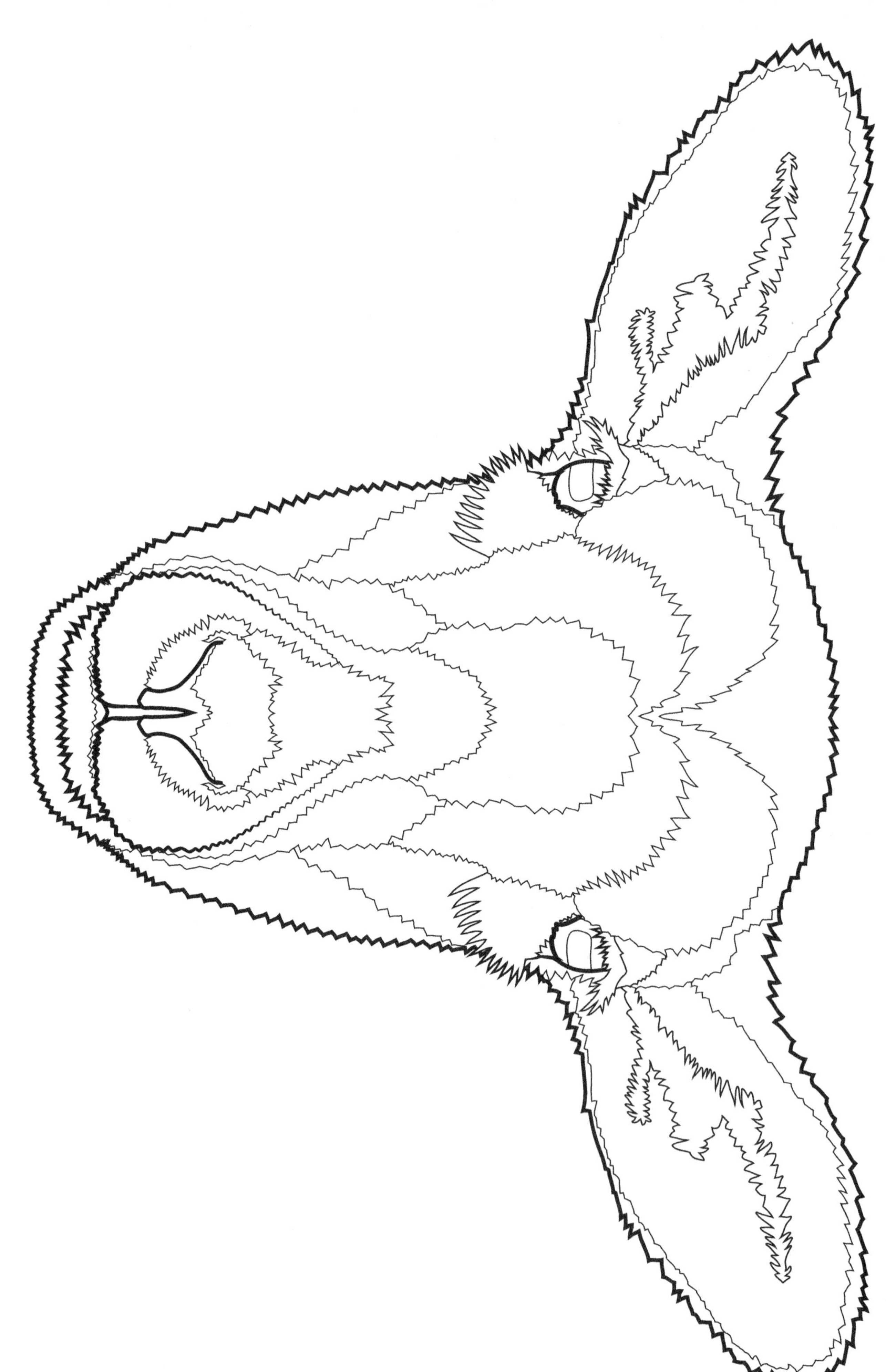

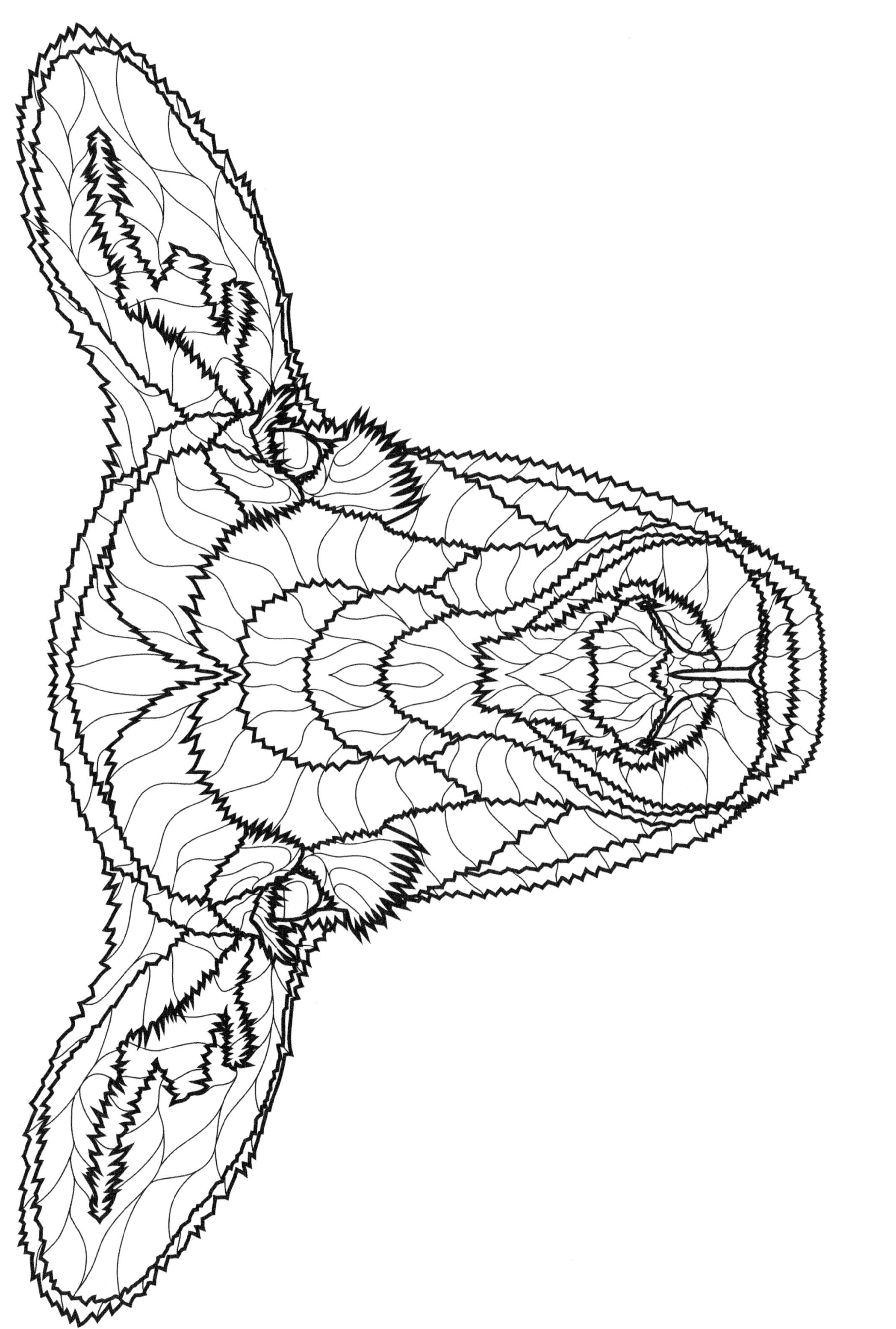

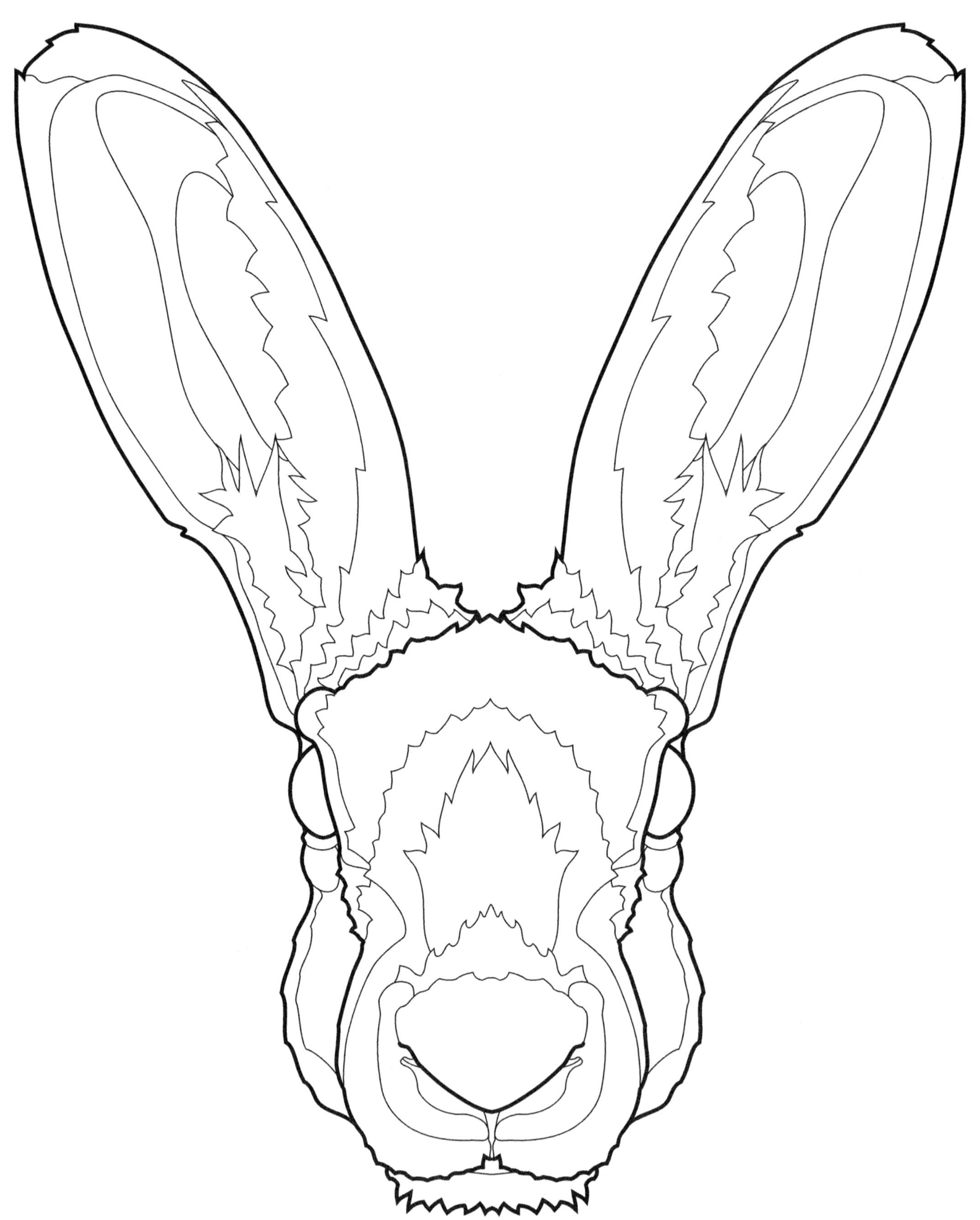

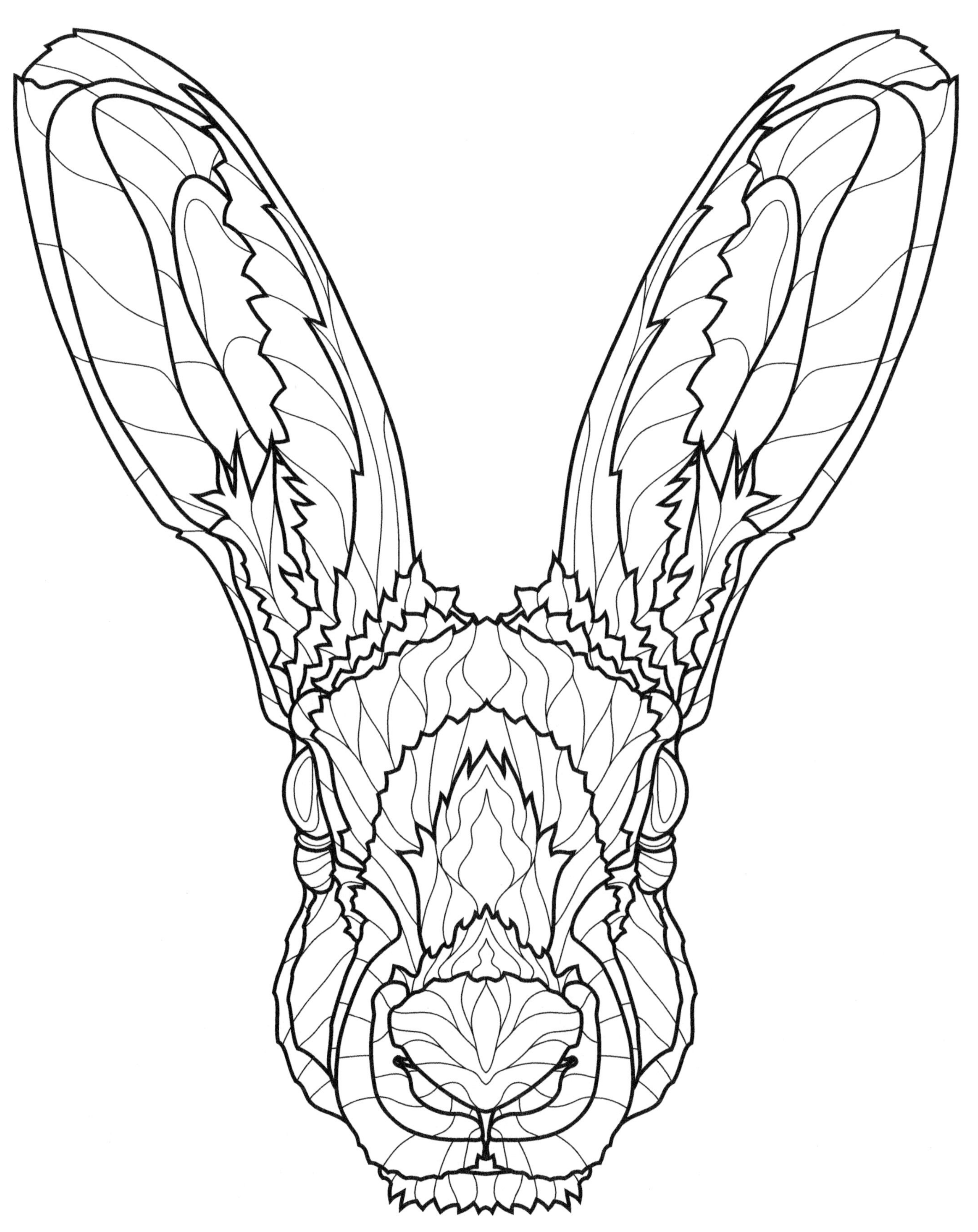

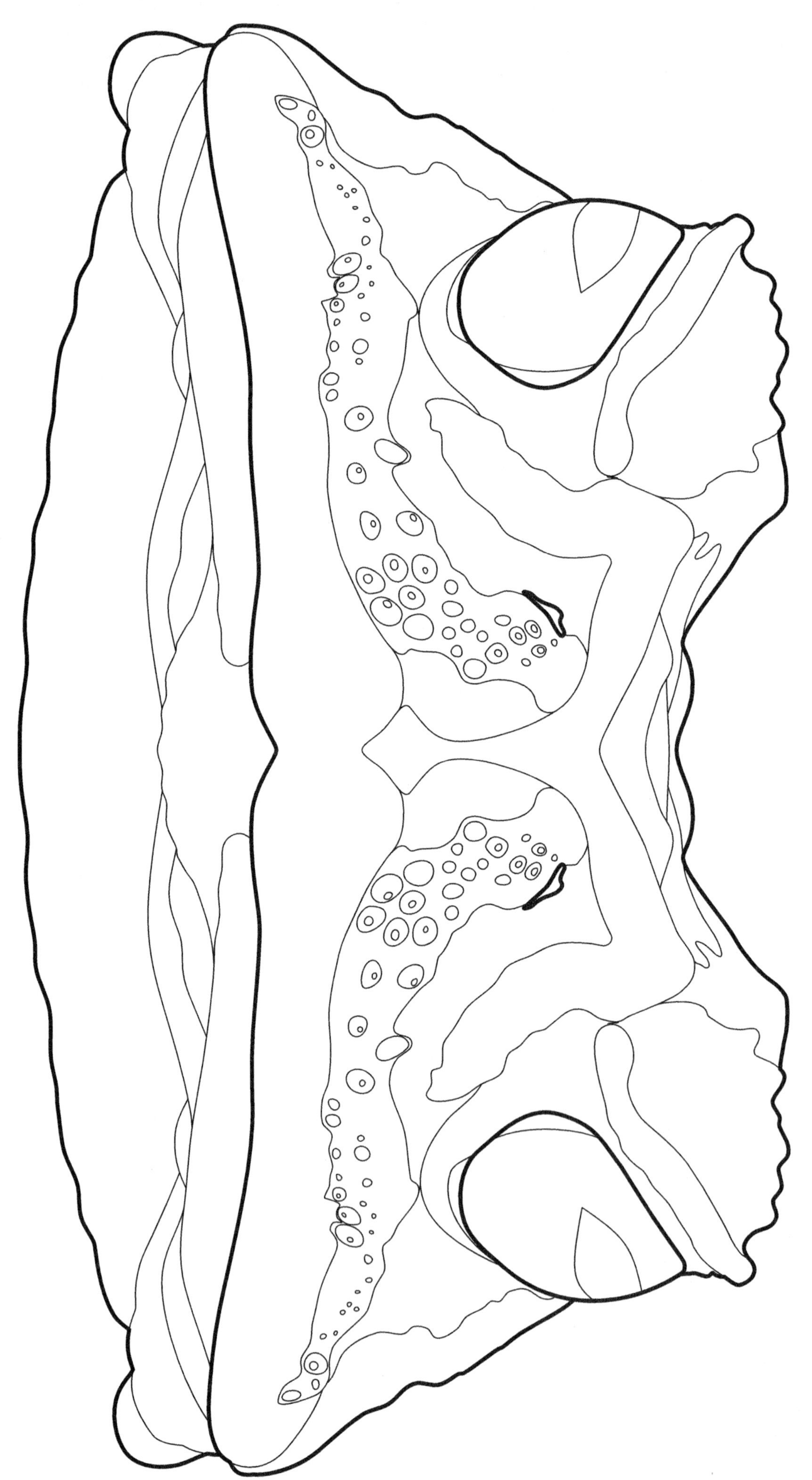

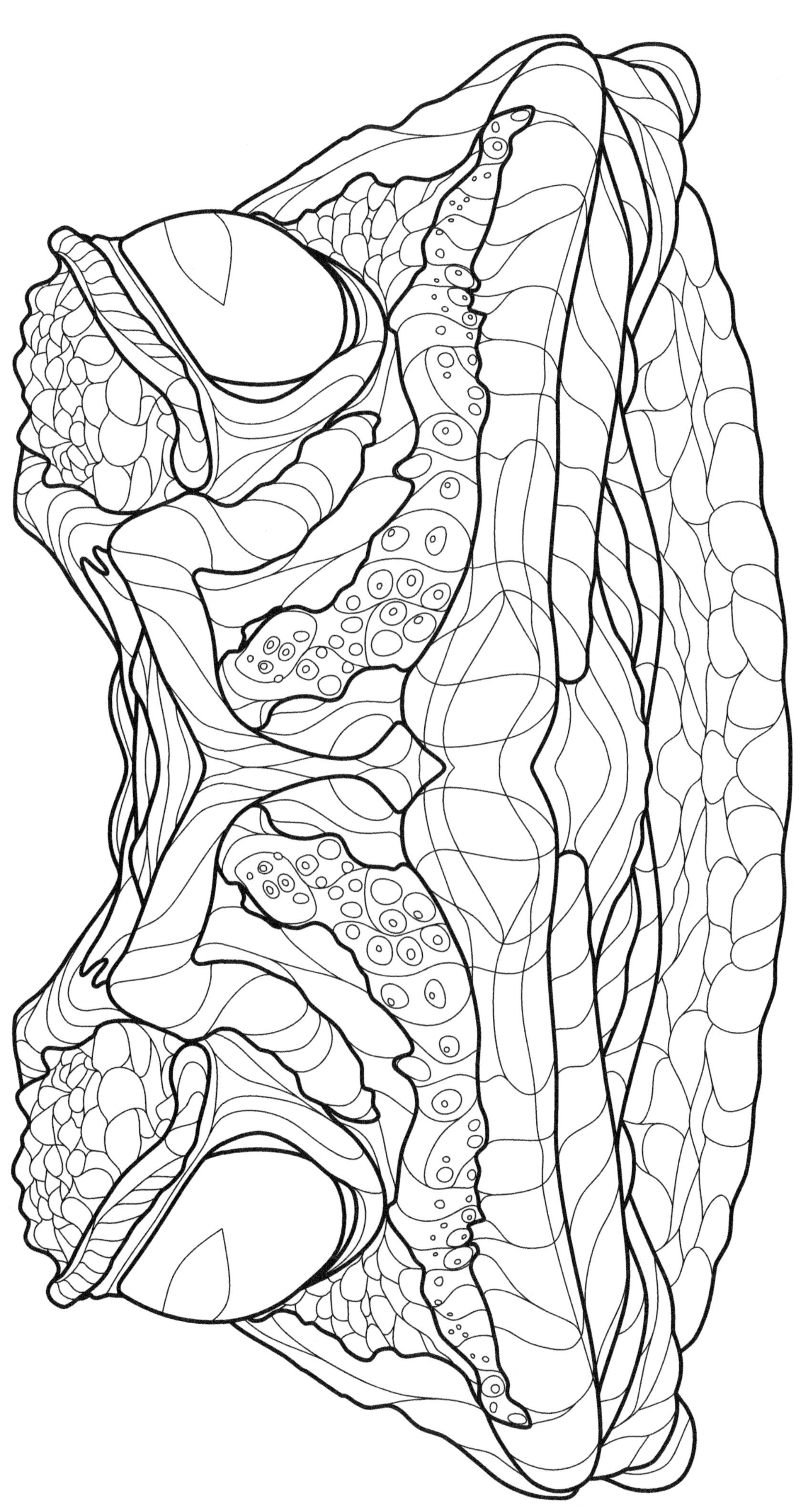

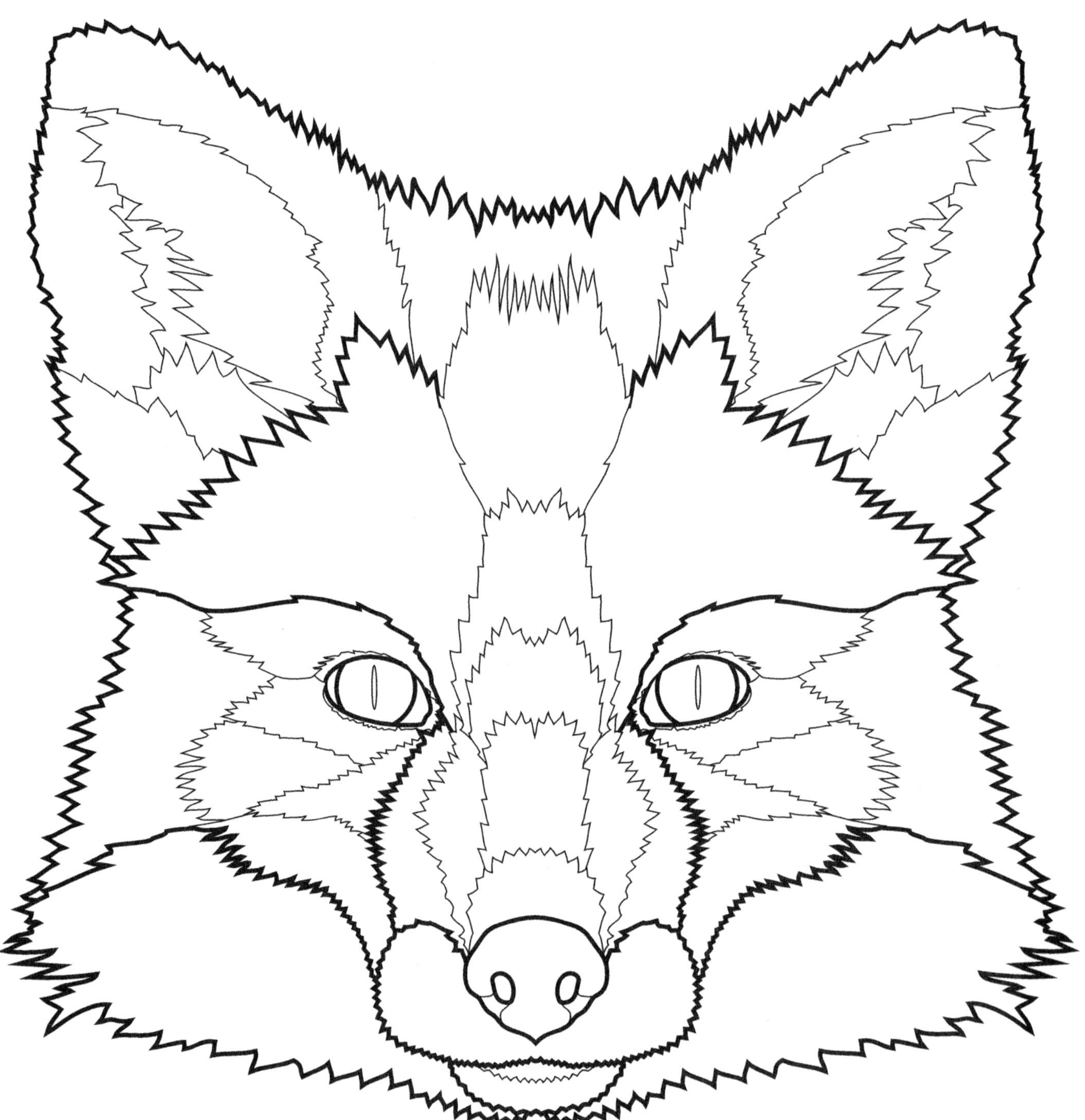

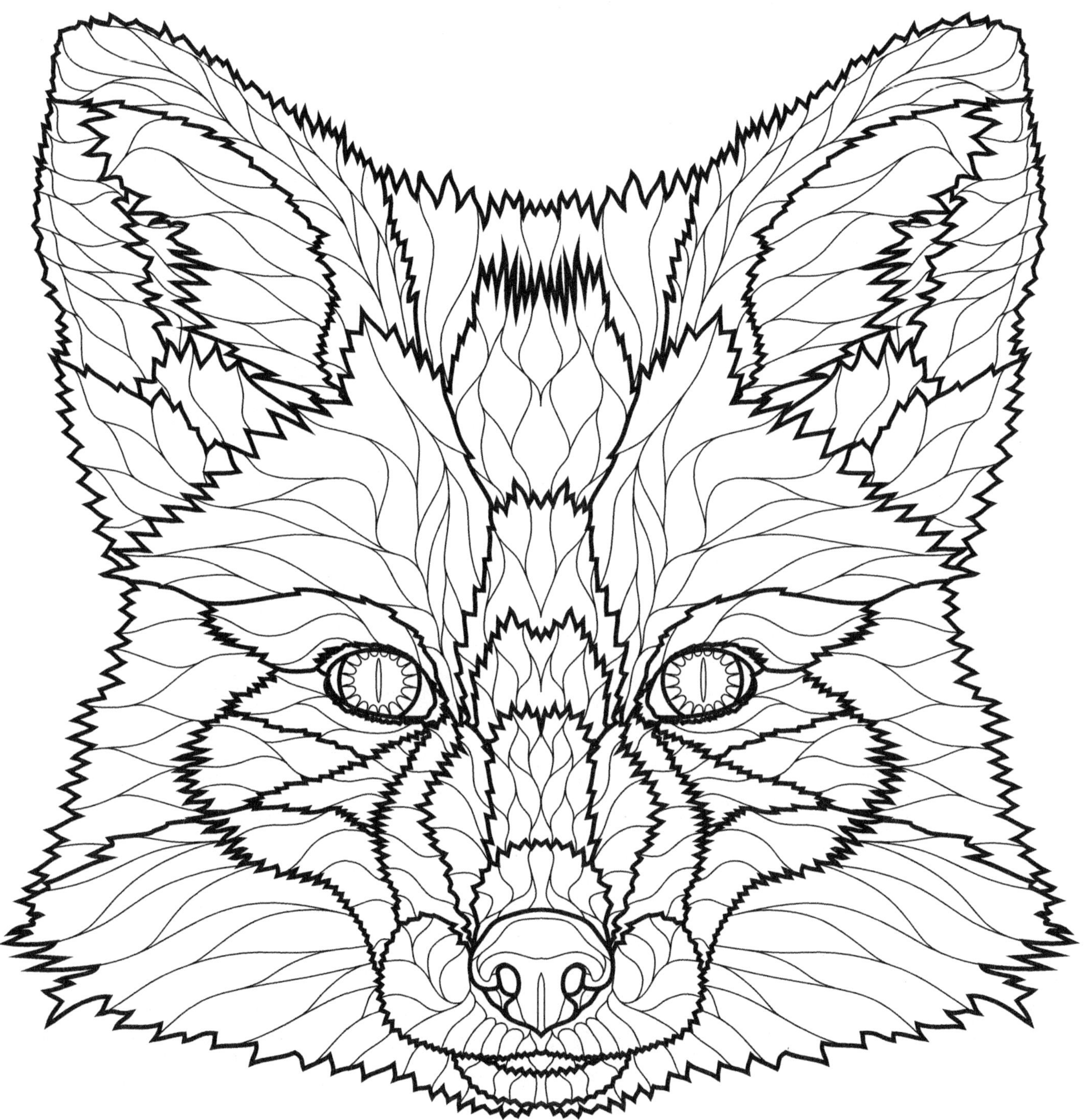

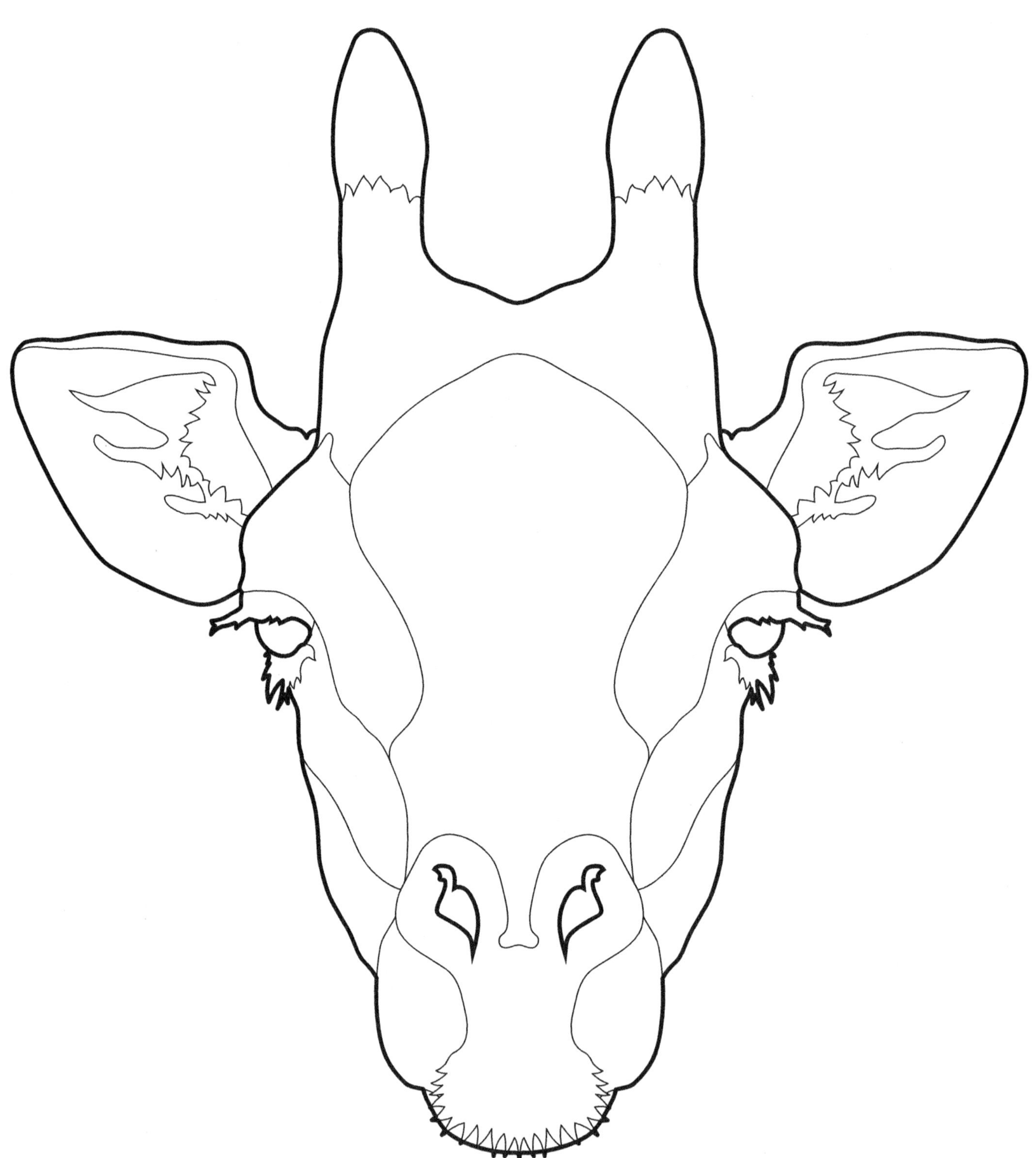

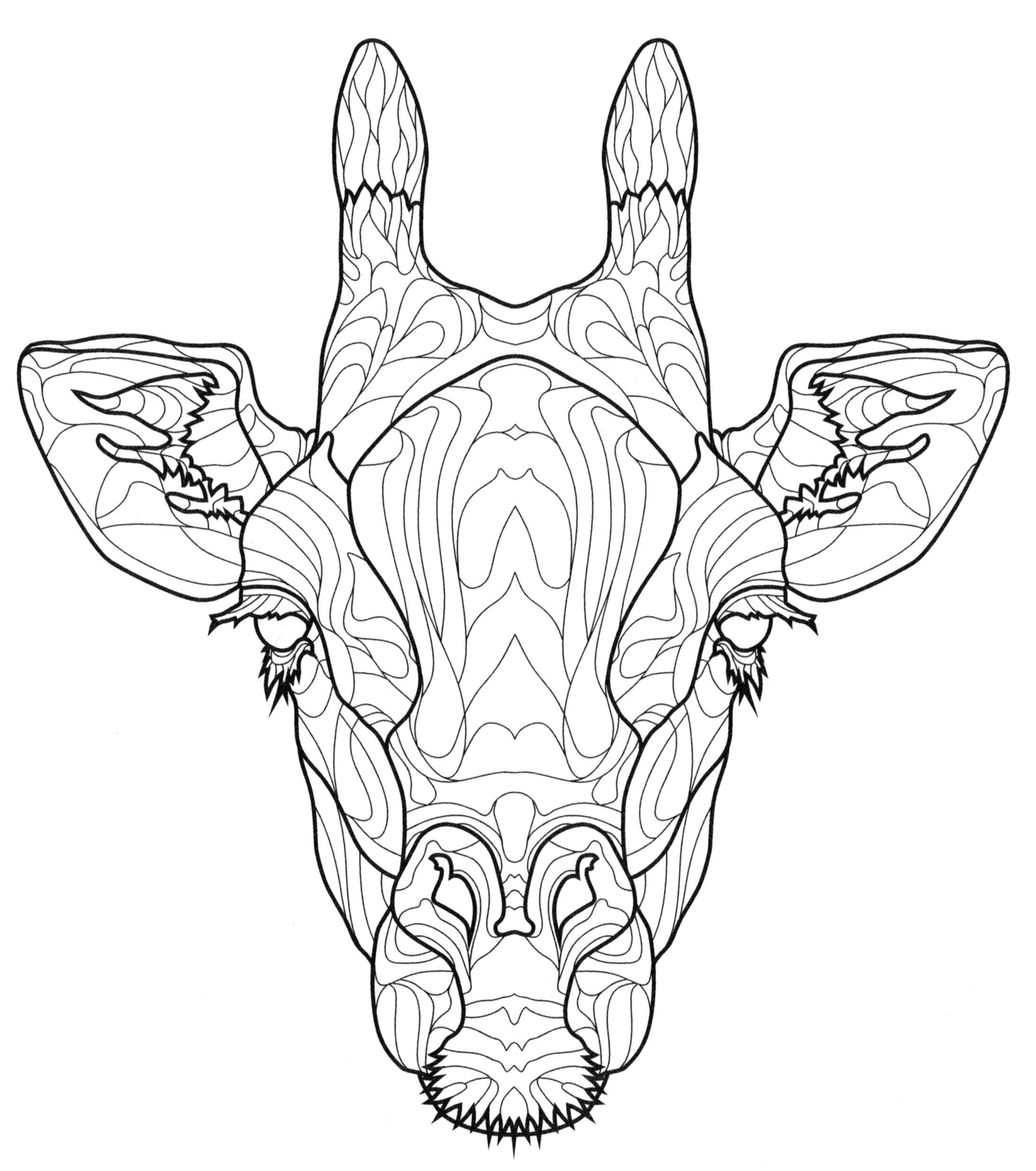

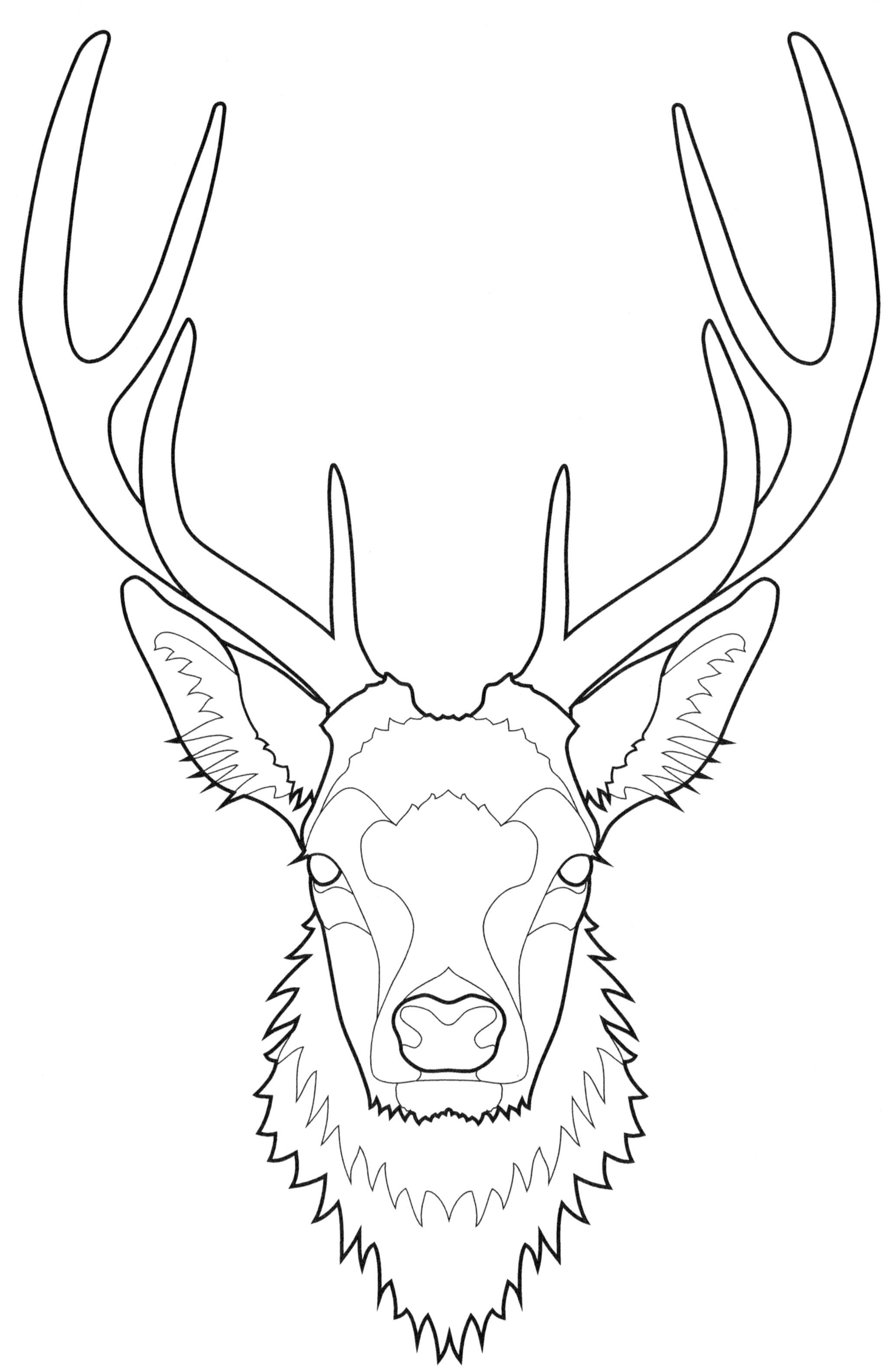

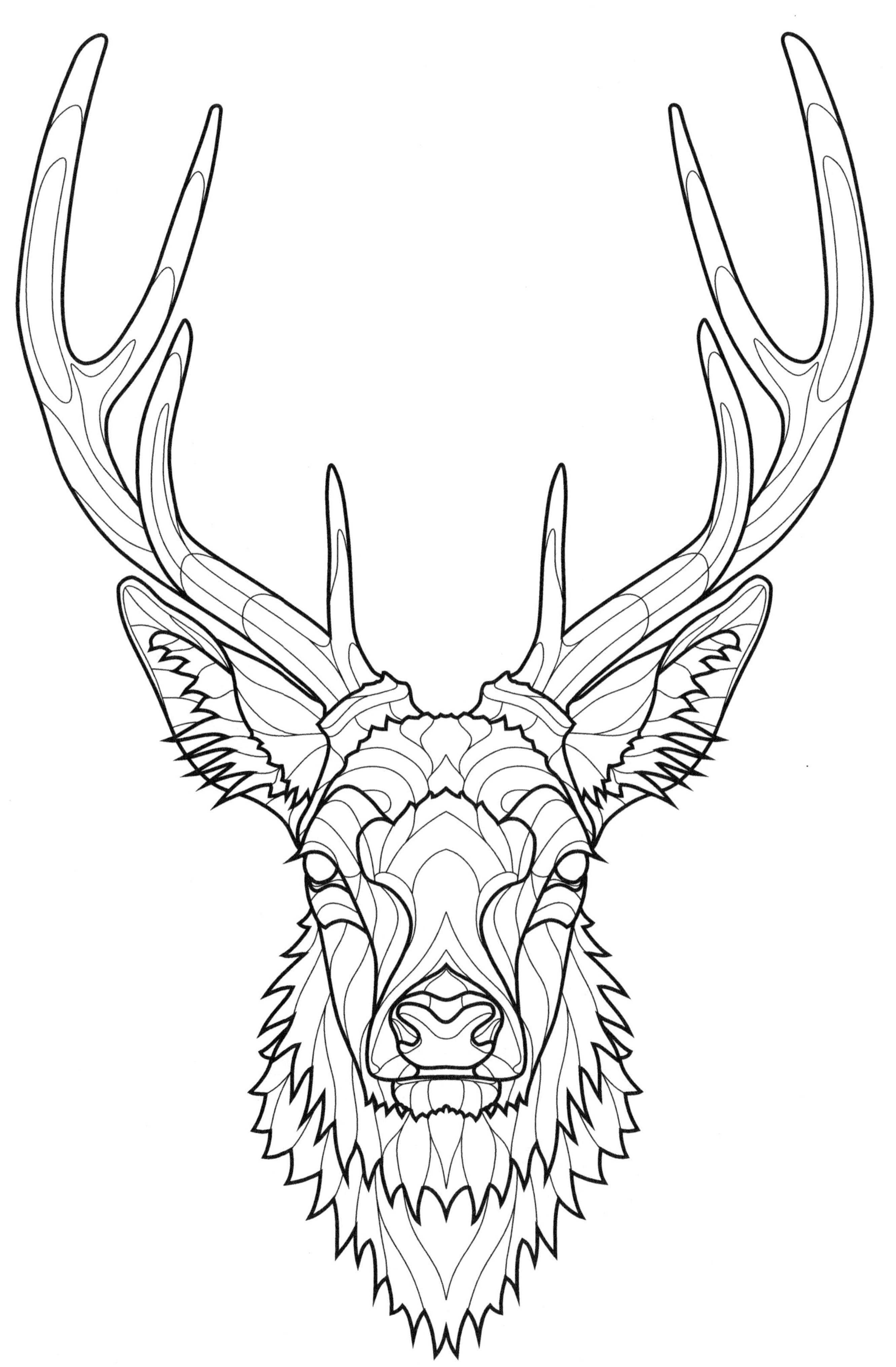

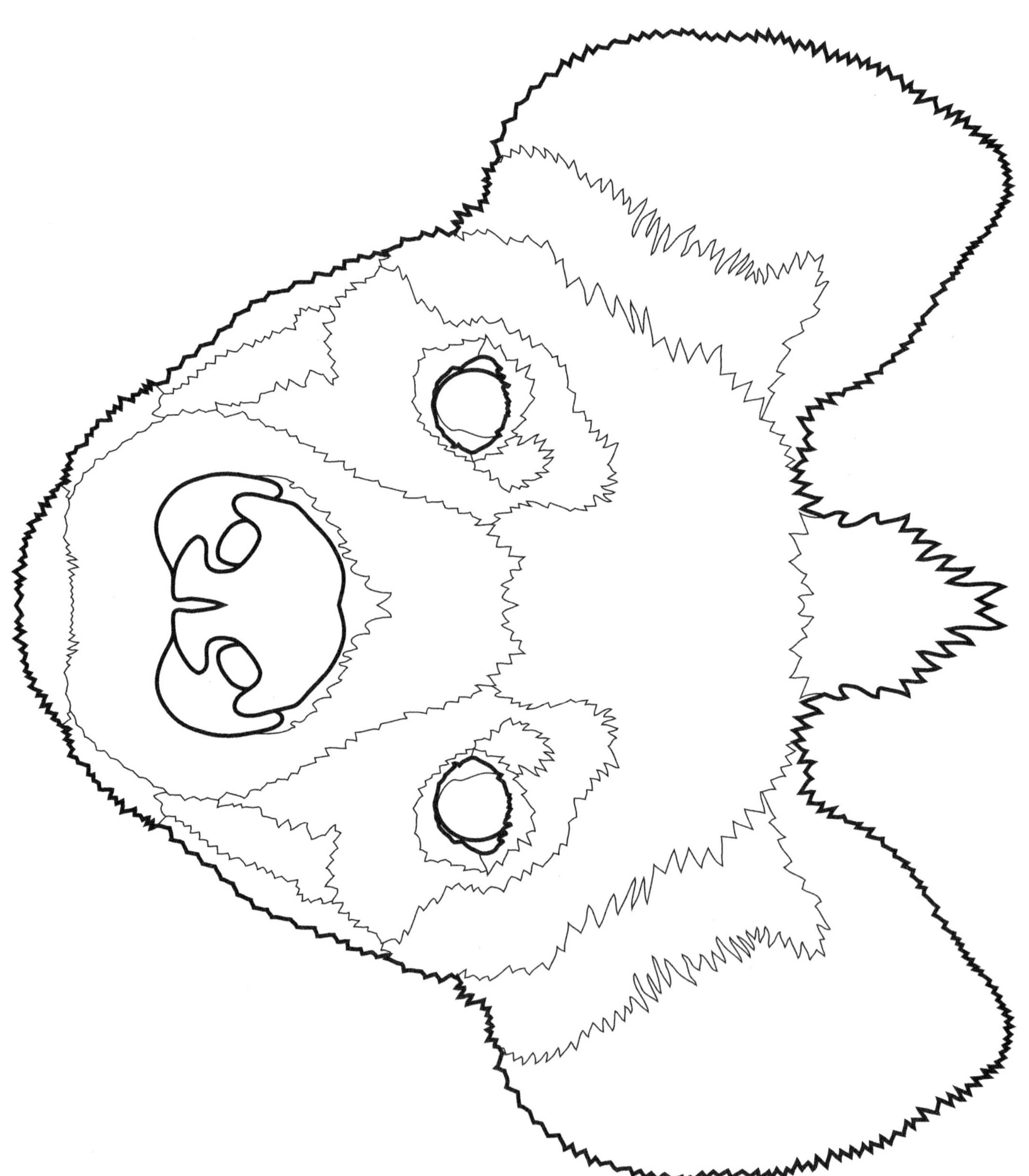

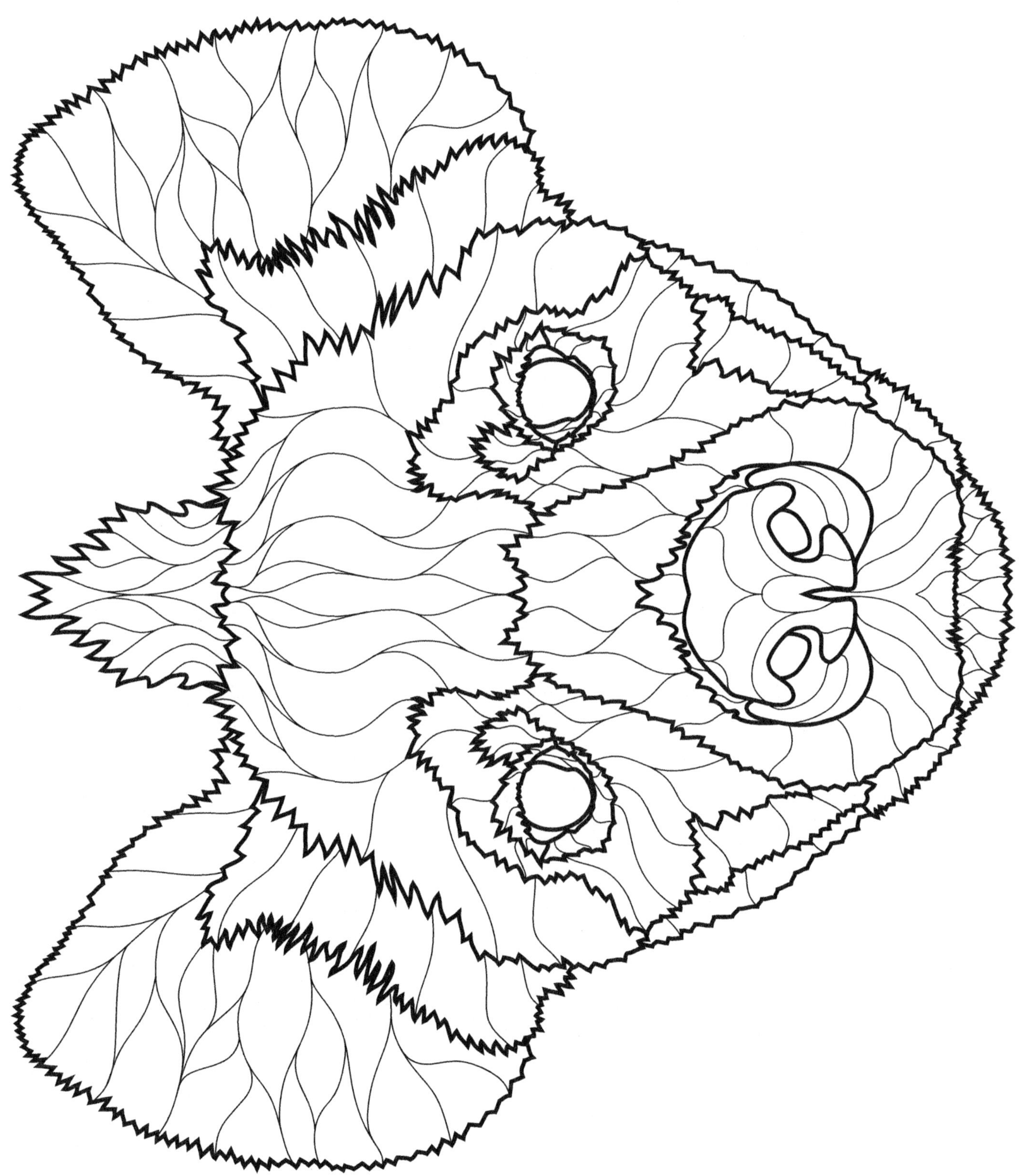

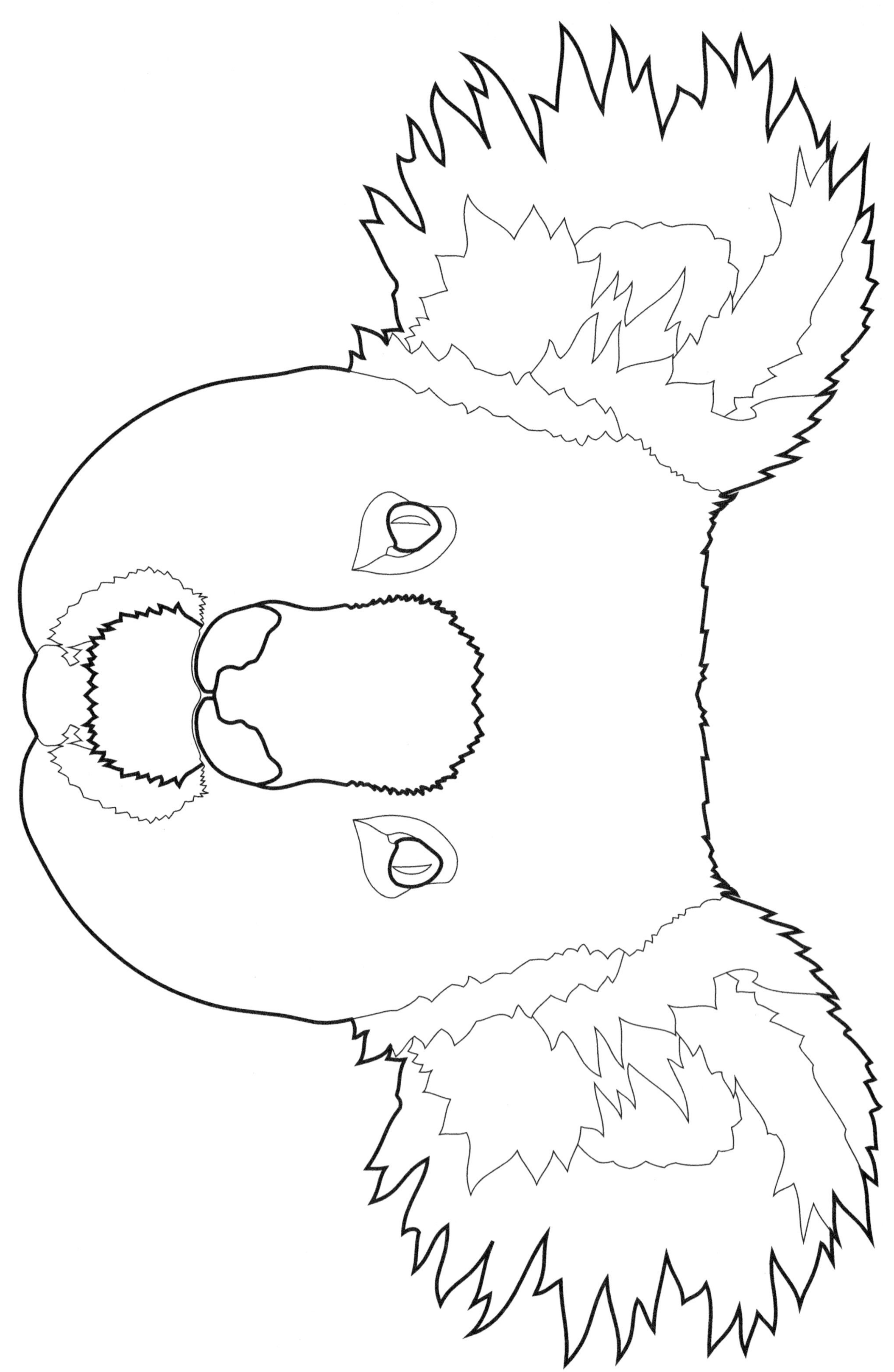

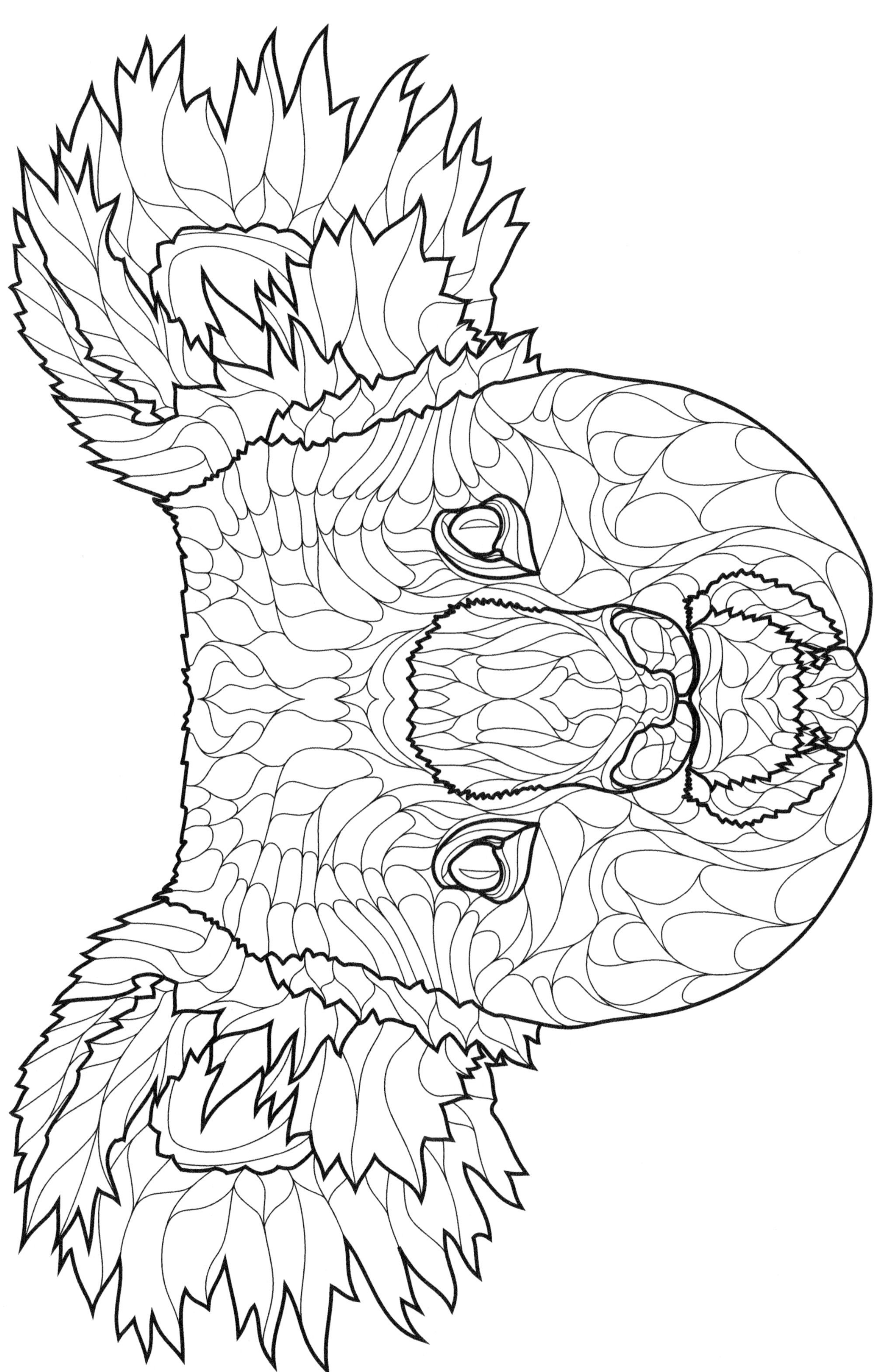

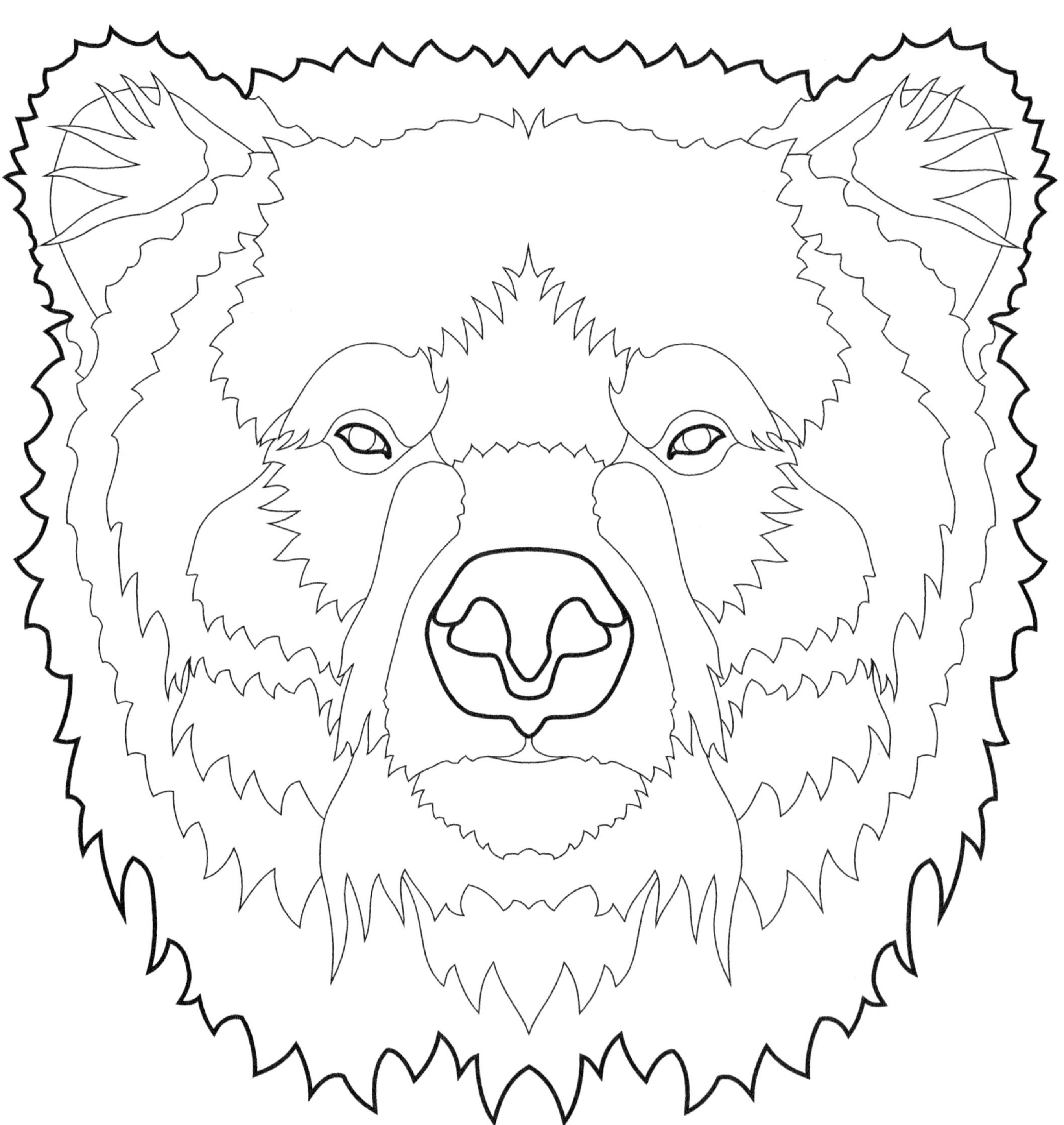

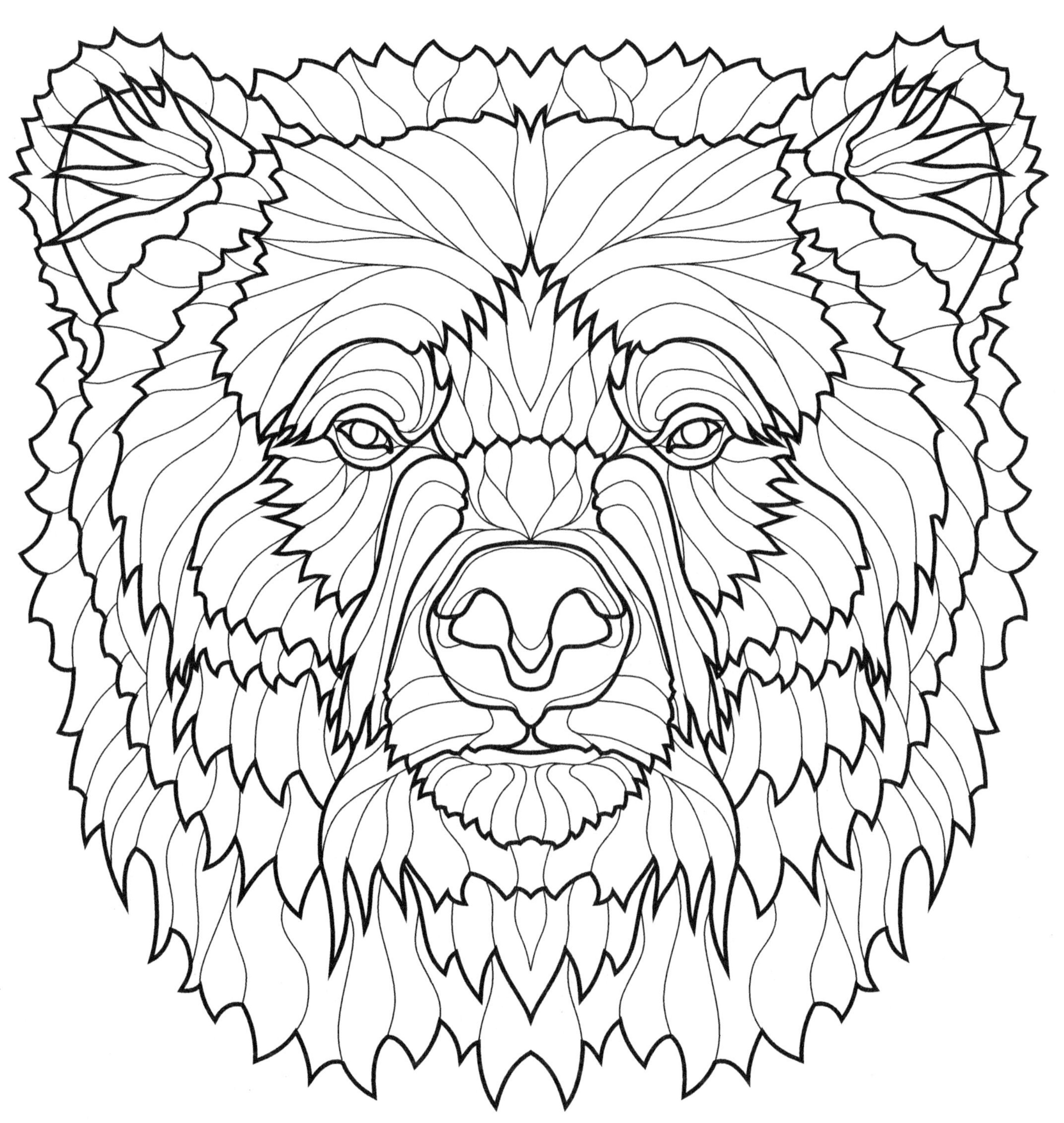

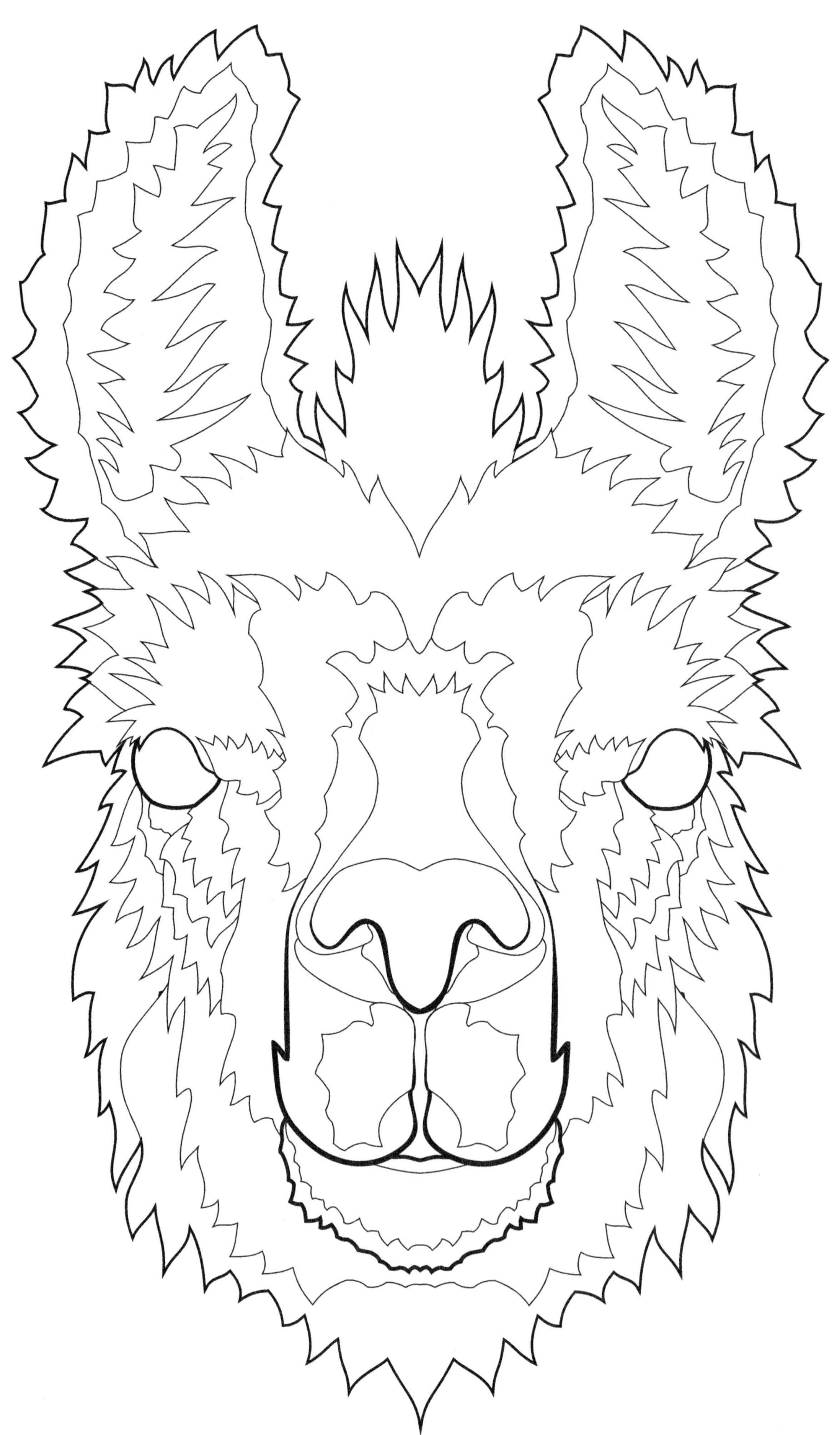

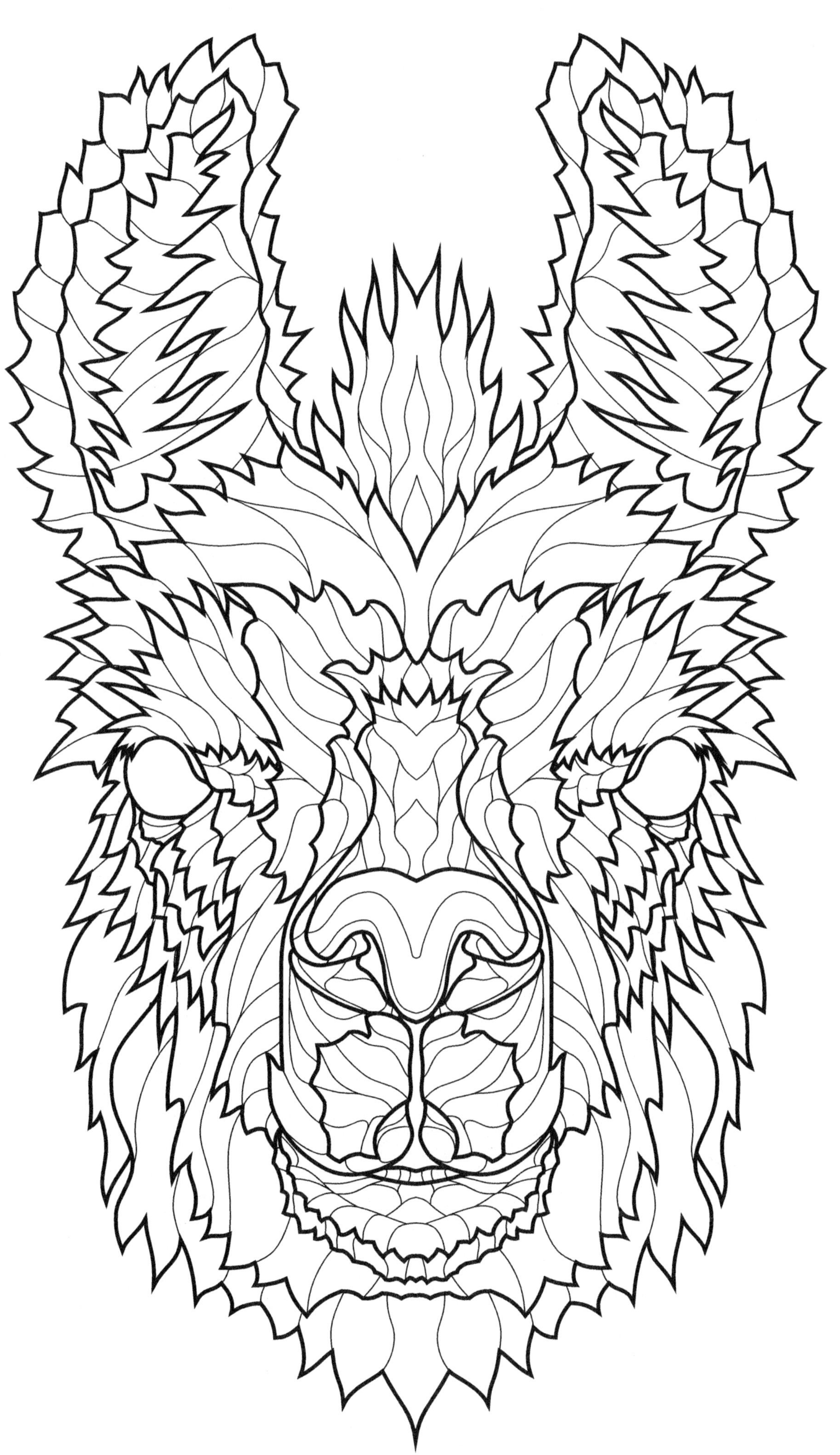

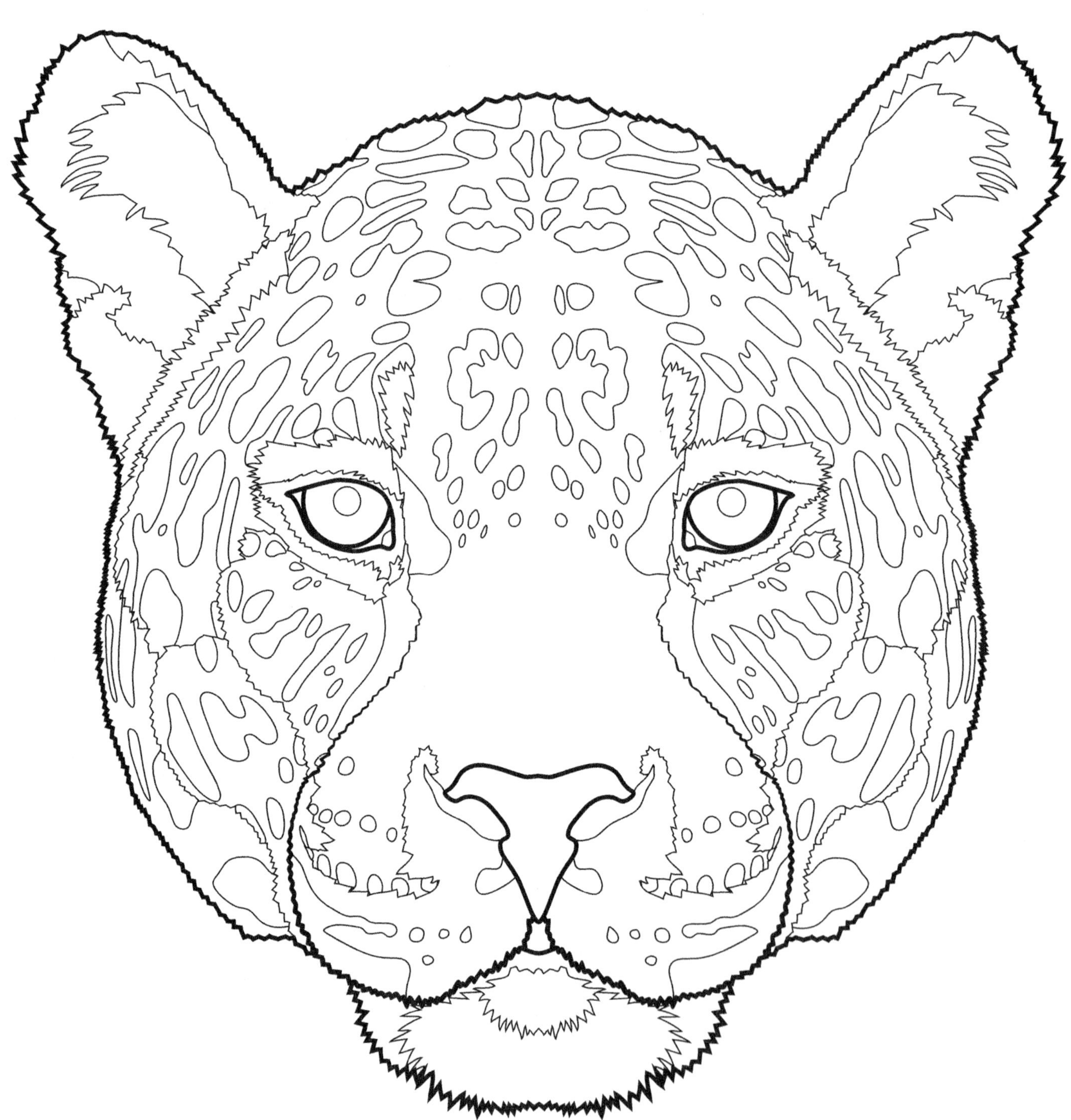

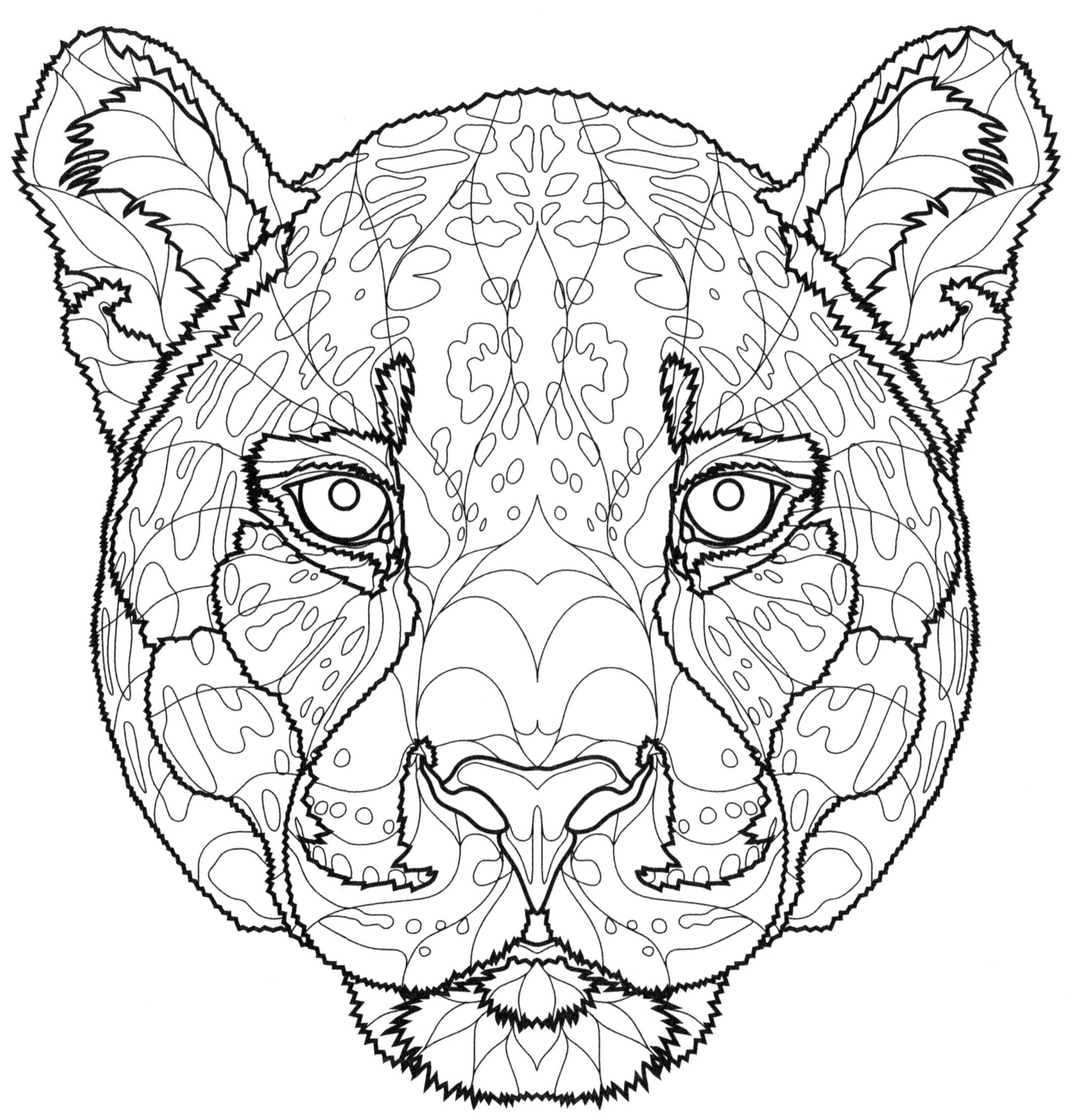

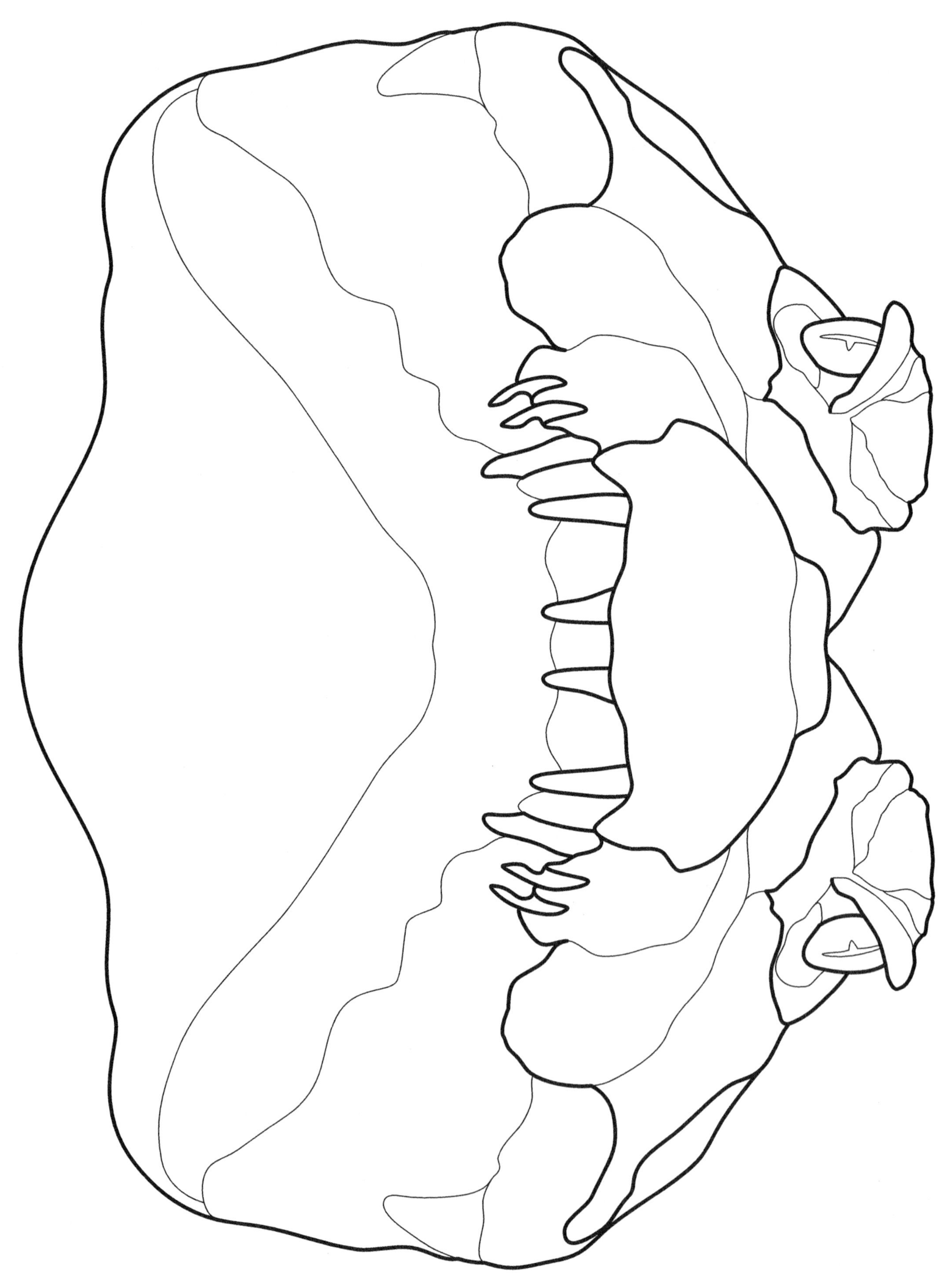

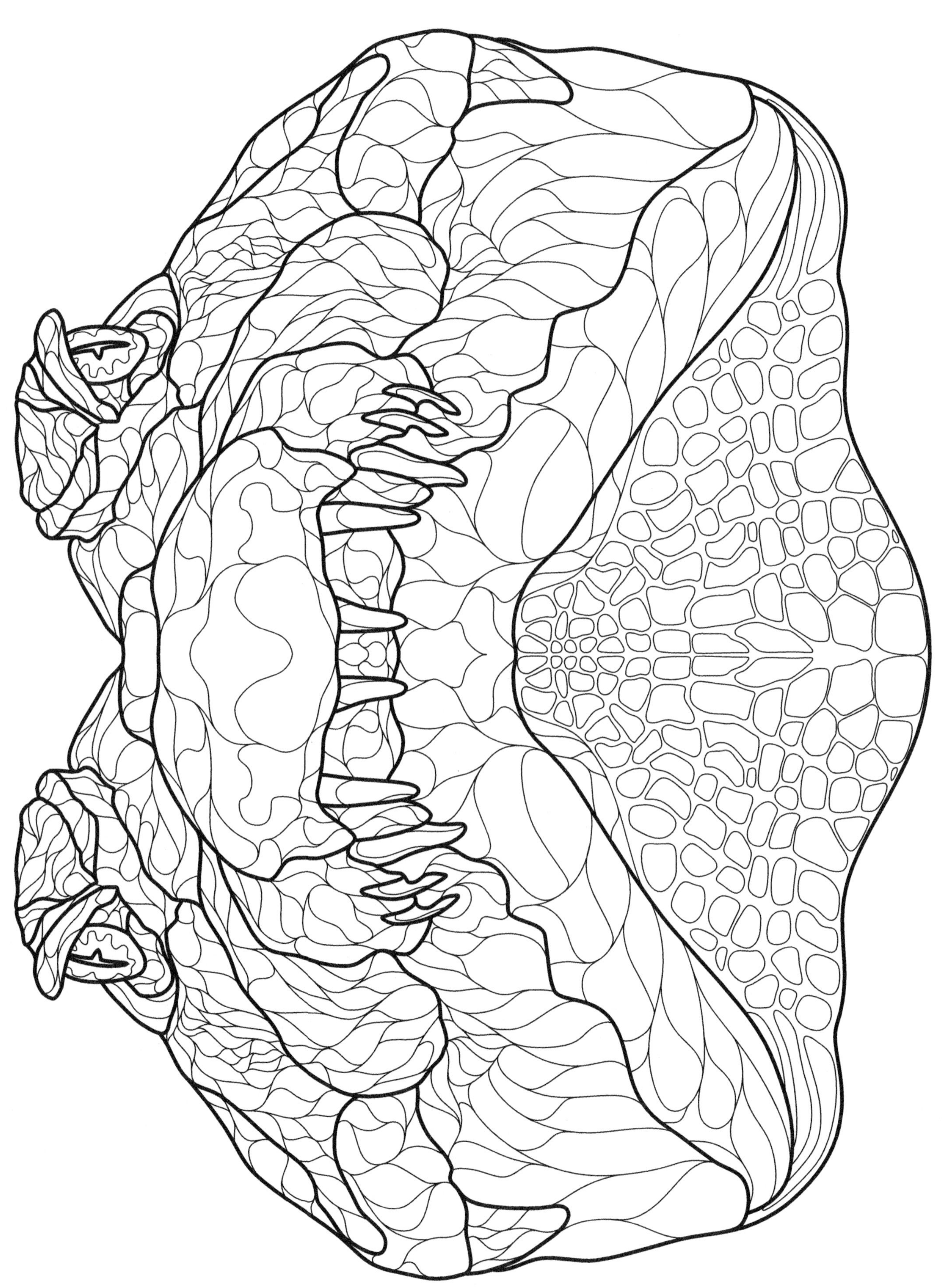

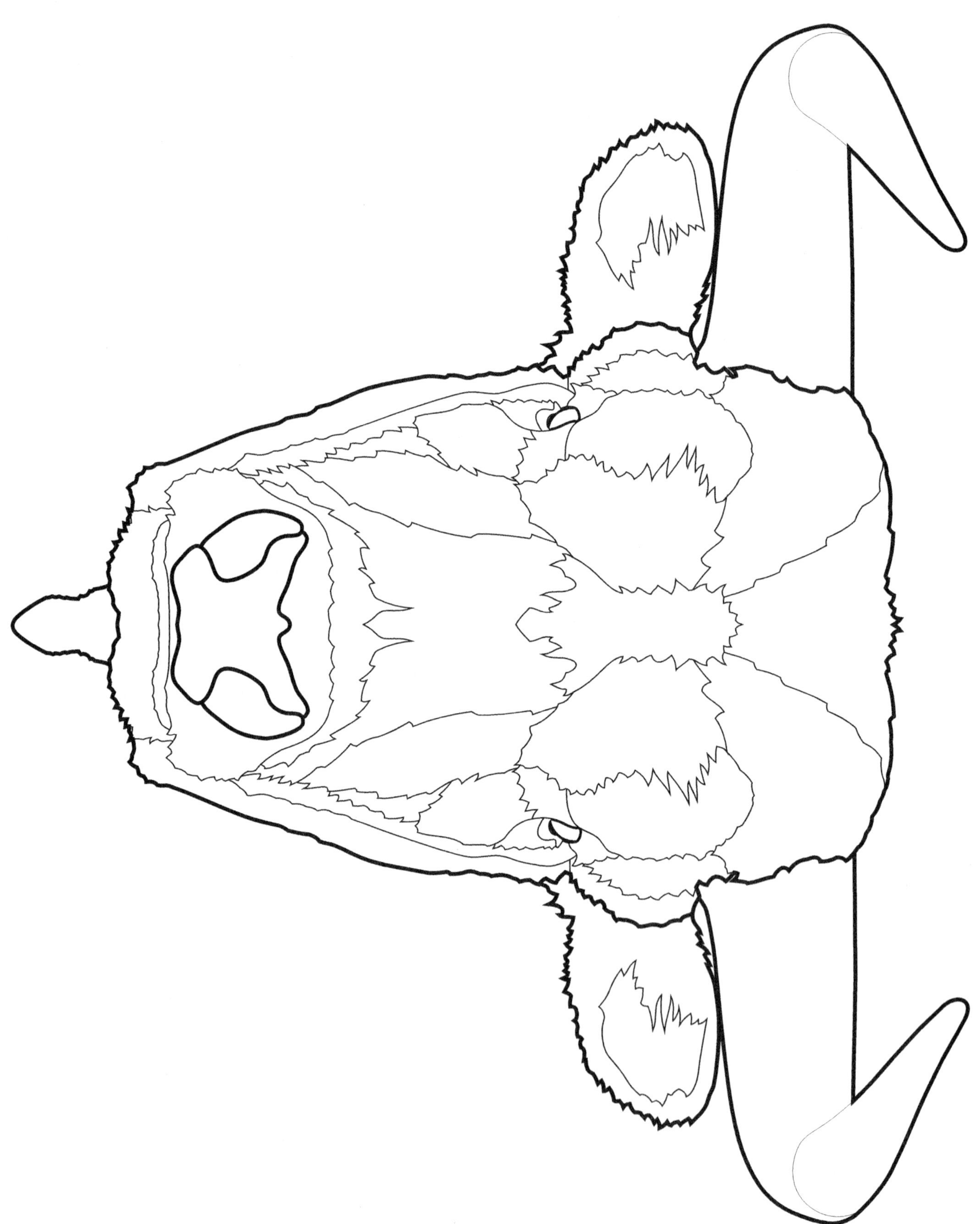

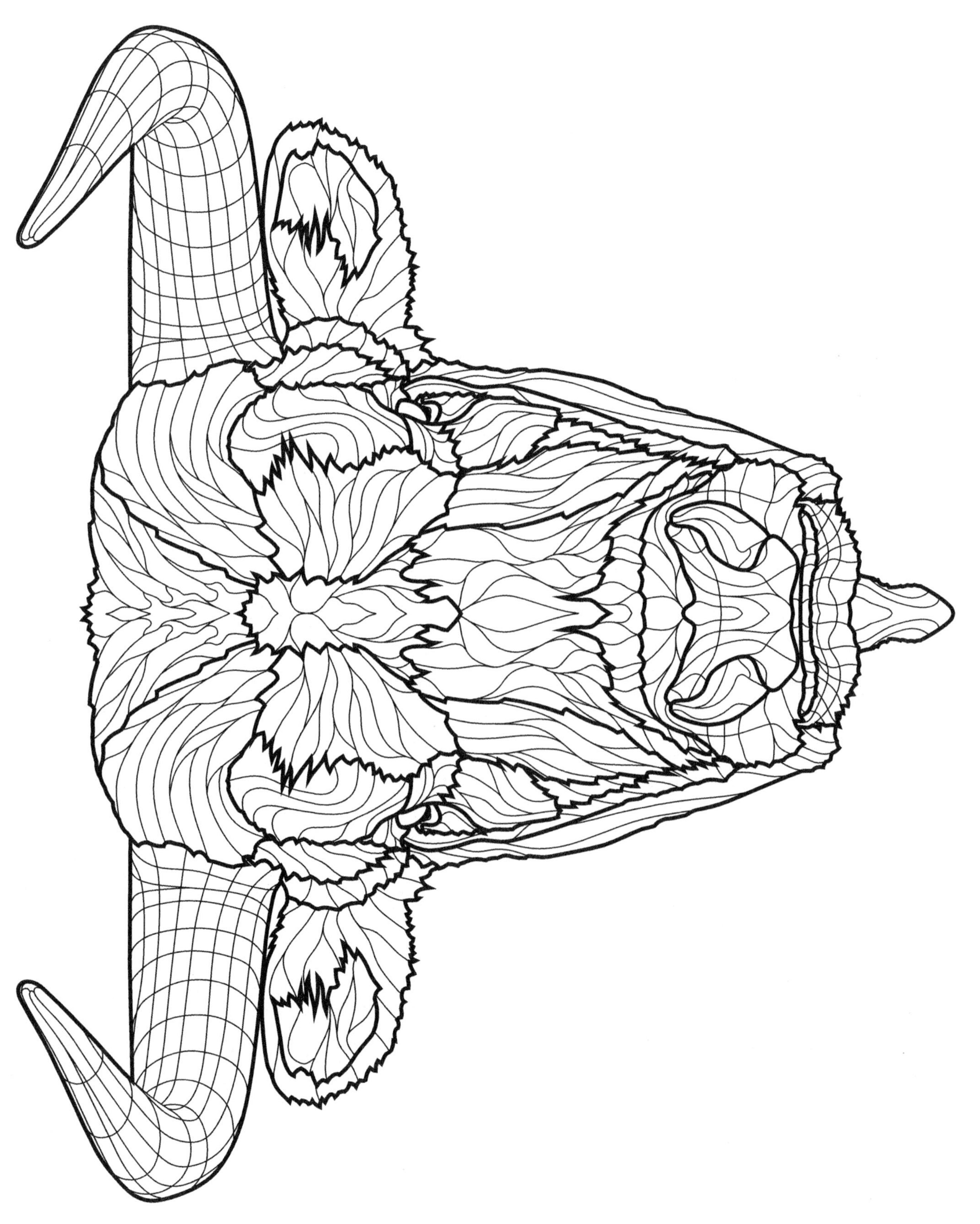

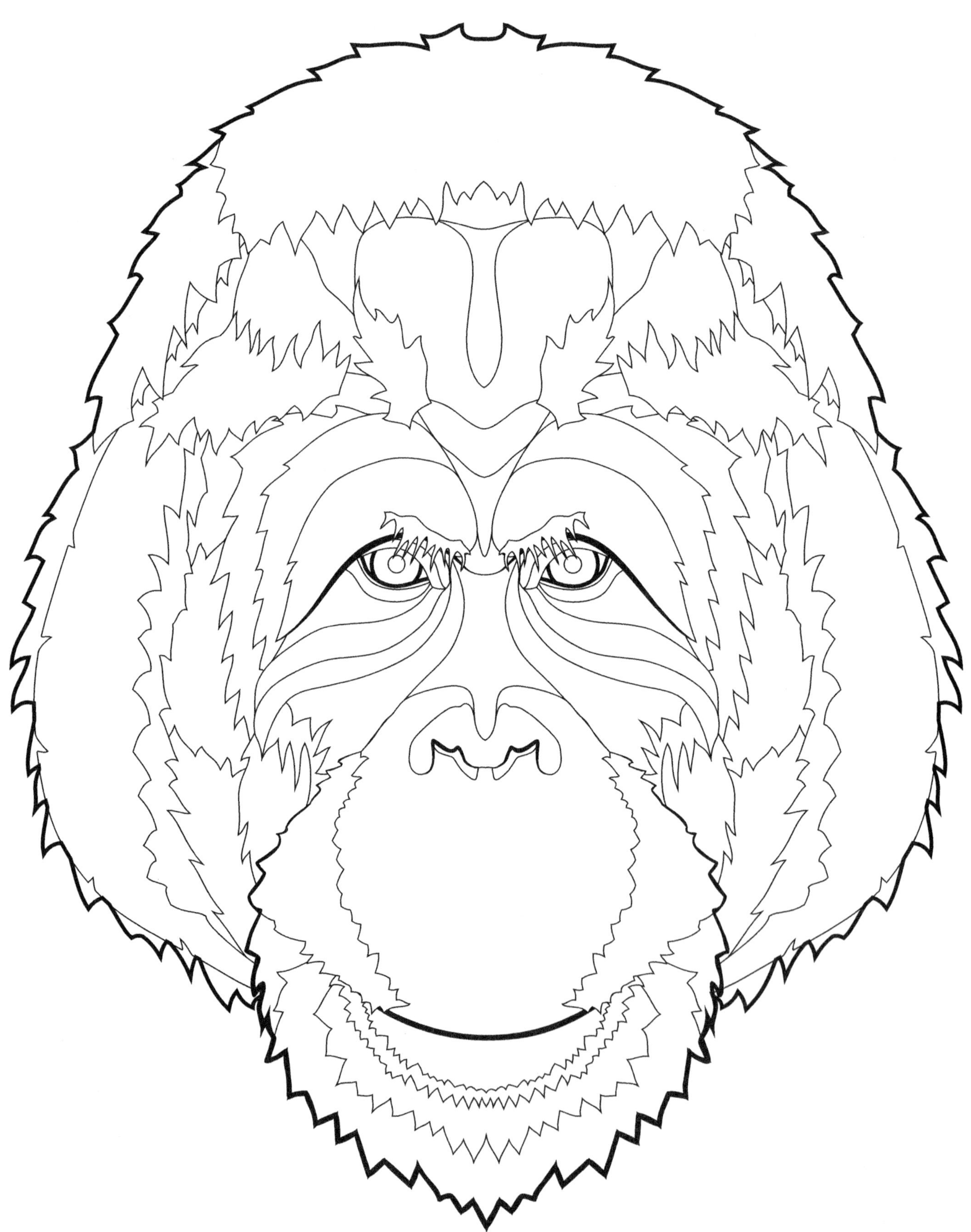

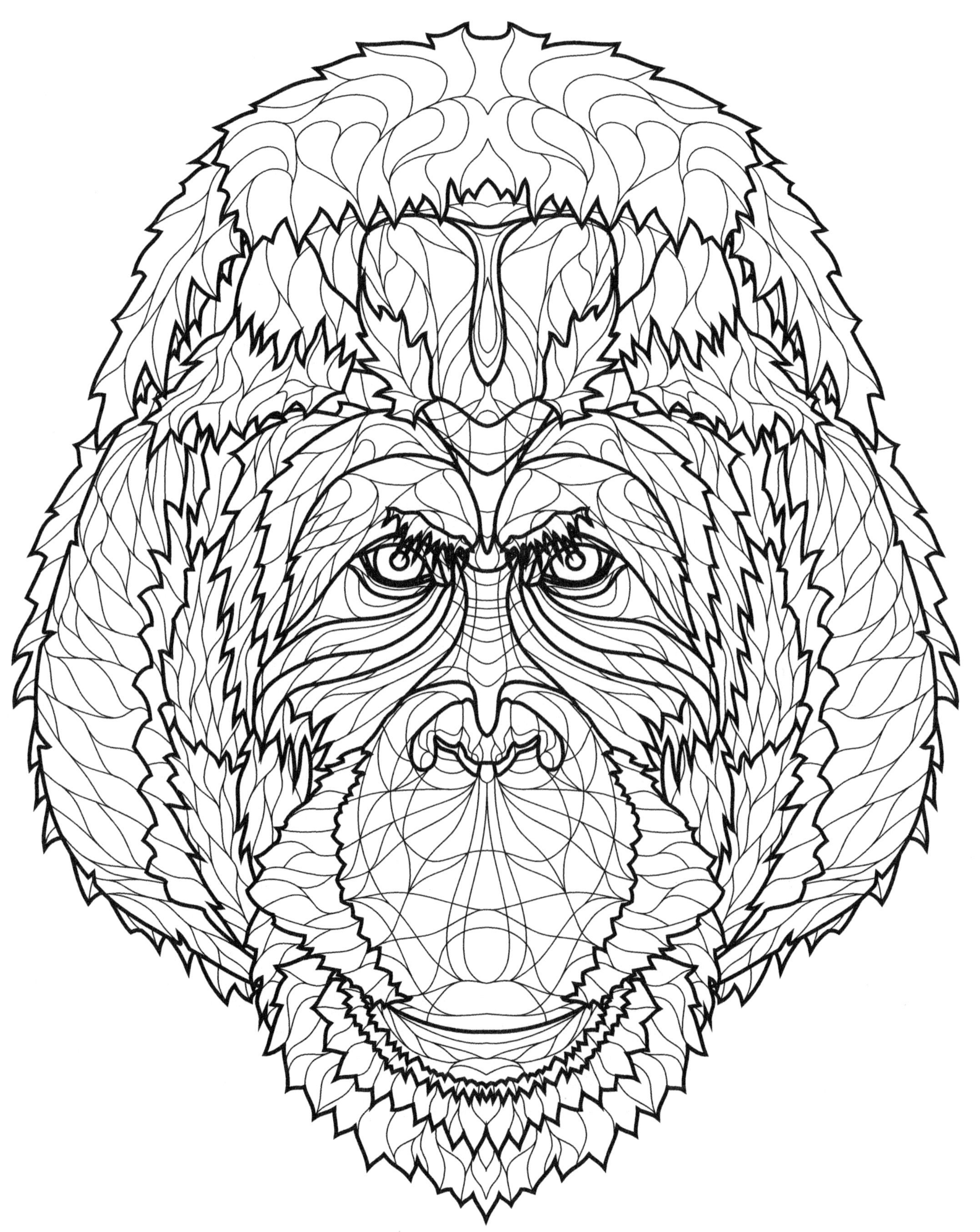

ANIMAL KINGDOM

Book II: Spirit

Bonus content from our next book

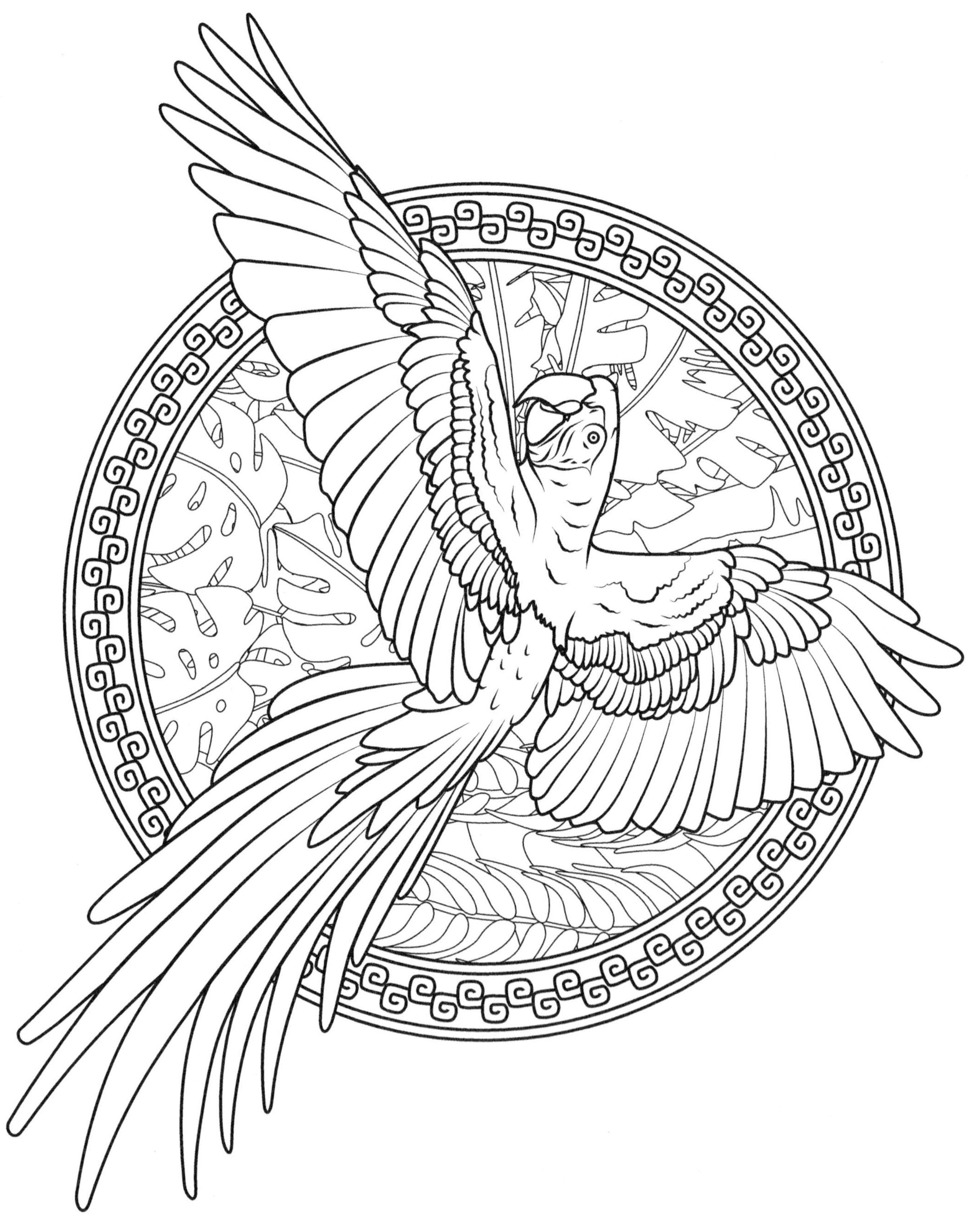

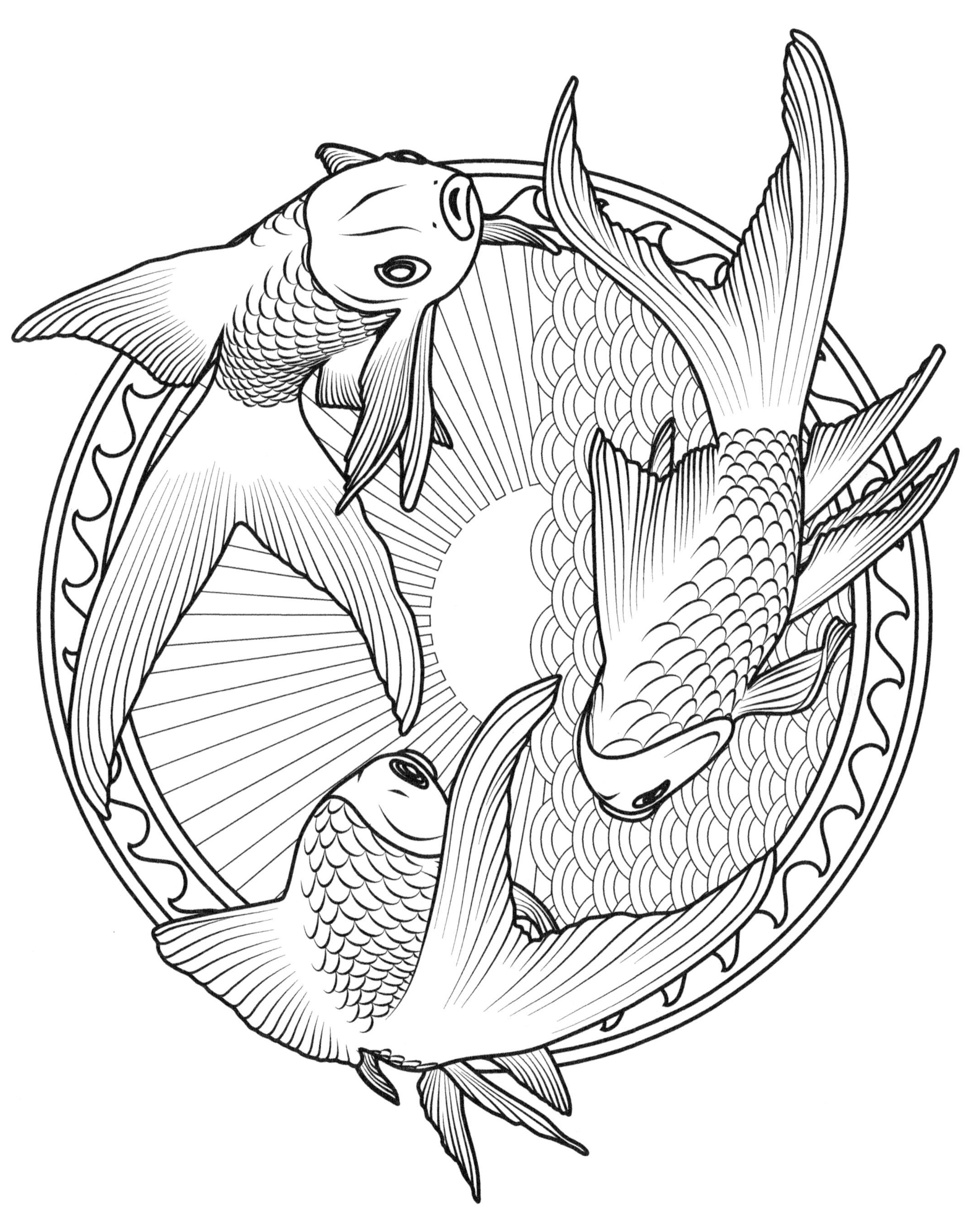

Printed in Great Britain
by Amazon

77483077R00093